# How to answer interview questions

*100 Smart Answers to the most asked questions.
Conquer the recruiter, show up your Best Skills and
succeed in the job hiring process.
Be prepared and Get that Job*

**By Donald Thomson**

© **Copyright 2019 - All rights reserved.**

The content contained within this book may not be reproduced, duplicated or transmitted without direct written permission from the author or the publisher.

Under no circumstances will any blame or legal responsibility be held against the publisher, or author, for any damages, reparation, or monetary loss due to the information contained within this book. Either directly or indirectly.

**Legal Notice:**

This book is copyright protected. This book is only for personal use. You cannot amend, distribute, sell, use, quote or paraphrase any part, or the content within this book, without the consent of the author or publisher.

**Disclaimer Notice:**

Please note the information contained within this document is for educational and entertainment purposes only. All effort has been executed to present accurate, up to date, and reliable, complete information. No warranties of any kind are declared or implied. Readers acknowledge that the author is not engaging in the rendering of legal, financial, medical or professional advice. The content within this book has been derived from various sources. Please consult a licensed professional before attempting any techniques outlined in this book.

By reading this document, the reader agrees that under no circumstances is the author responsible for any losses, direct or indirect, which are incurred as a result of the use of information contained within this document, including, but not limited to, — errors, omissions, or inaccuracies.

# Abstract

The book is coordinated to individuals who are searching for a job and are going to confront a job interview. The book contains the 100 most regular inquiries that scout could pose to the applicant. The objective is to show individuals how to confront a focusing on circumstance like a job interview, being as of now arranged on the most plausible inquiries they can get, so as to make them loose and agreeable. Interviews can appear to be frightening, yet even a restless or a bashful individual can improve their interviewing aptitudes incredibly just by setting up a couple of days ahead of time. Perusing this book is, as of now, a decent initial step, Read on for pragmatic interviewing tips, and instances of what to state.

# Introduction

In any event, when you have gone on a greater number of interviews than you can tally, job interviewing never appears to get any simpler. With each job interview, you are meeting new individuals, selling yourself and your abilities, and frequently getting an exhaustive round of questions about what you know or don't have a clue. What's more, you have to remain energetic and excited about everything. This can be a test, particularly when you're interviewing for a job you couldn't want anything more than to get employed for. So, there are approaches to make a job interview feel considerably less unpleasant. Only a little preparation time can go far. The additional time you take ahead of time to prepare, the more agreeable you'll feel during the genuine interview. Keep in mind, however, that a job interview isn't a test: you don't have to read for a considerable length of time. Or maybe, you simply need to do due to persistence in investigating the organization, see precisely what they are searching for in another contract and guarantee that you're ready to examine your experience and what makes you an extraordinary fit for the job.

# Table of **Contents**

MEANING OF INTERVIEW ..................................................... 1

TYPES OF INTERVIEWS ........................................................ 2

    BASED ON THE COUNT OF PEOPLE INVOLVED ............ 2

        One-to one interview (Personal interview): ..................... 2

        Group interview: ................................................................ 2

        Panel interview (Committee Interview): ........................... 3

    BASED ON THE PLANNING INVOLVED ............................ 3

        A structured interview (Formal interview or guided interview): ........................................................................... 3

        Unstructured interview (Informal interview or conversational interview): ..................................................... 4

    BASED ON JUDGING THE ABILITIES; ............................. 4

        Behavioral-based interview: .............................................. 4

        Problem-solving interview (Task-Oriented interview): ... 5

        Depth interview (In-depth interview): ............................. 5

        Stress interview: ................................................................ 6

    BASED ON THE TASK ......................................................... 6

        Apprenticeship interview: ................................................. 6

        Evaluation interview: ........................................................ 7

        Promotion interview: ........................................................ 7

Counseling interview: .................................................... 7

Disciplinary interview: .................................................. 7

Persuasive interview: ................................................... 8

## OBJECTIVES OF INTERVIEW: .............................................. 9

Do your research ....................................................... 10

Dress sharp ............................................................. 11

Be punctual ............................................................. 12

Make your selling points clear .......................................... 12

Speak the right body language ........................................... 12

Be Succinct (and Definitely, Don't Recite Your Resume) .. 13

Follow-Up After the Interview ........................................... 14

## THE TOP 100 COMMON QUESTIONS ............................................ 15

### FIVE MOST COMMON QUESTIONS ........................................... 15

1. Tell me about yourself ............................................... 15
2. Describe yourself .................................................... 16
3. Why should we choose you? ............................................ 17
4. What are your strengths? ............................................. 17
5. What are your weaknesses? ............................................ 18

### QUESTIONS ON YOUR PERSON .............................................. 19

6. What is your dream? .................................................. 19
7. How do you relieve stress? ........................................... 20

8. How would you feel about having a younger boss? 20

9. Among the personal interests, you have the reading: what is the last book you have read? ................................... 21

10. Which is your favorite book ................................. 22

11. How do you evaluate success? ............................. 22

12. What are the characteristics of a good boss, according to you? ............................................................. 24

13. What do you do in your spare time? ..................... 25

14. How do you like working? ................................... 26

15. Describe to me a situation in which you put your skills into practice! ............................................................. 27

16. Do you work well under stress? ............................ 28

17. How do you work in a team? ................................ 29

18. Do you prefer to work alone or in a team? ............ 30

19. Which role do you play in a team? ....................... 31

20. If you asked your friends to describe you, what is the adjective I would hear most often? ................................ 31

21. Which person is a source of inspiration for you? .. 32

22. Tell me about something not on your resume. ... 33

23. What is your favorite quote? ............................... 34

24. What is your spiritual practice? .......................... 34

25. What do you do to improve yourself? ..................... 35

QUESTIONS AND SKILLS AND EXPERIENCE ............... 36

26. Tell me about your past experiences .................. 36

27. What are your greatest successes? ......................... 37

28. What kind of qualifications do you have? .......... 38

29. Why didn't you work this year? ......................... 38

30. I see you have no experience in the [any] field? 39

31. What did you do when you disagreed with your superiors? ..................................................................... 39

32. Tell me the last mistake you made ..................... 40

33. Why have you been fired? ...................................... 41

34. Have you had any volunteering experience? ...... 42

35. Have you built long-lasting friendships in your previous jobs? ................................................................ 43

36. Aren't you too qualified for this role? ................. 44

37. Was there a person who made the difference in your career? 45

38. What was the most boring job of your career? ... 46

39. Why did you choose your field of study? ............ 47

40. Can you describe a complex problem you had to solve?    49

41. What was your most significant accomplishment in your previous job? .................................................................. 50

42. Do you take any work home if you have not finished it ......................................................................................... 51

43. Have built a long-lasting relationship in your previous work ............................................................................... 52

QUESTIONS ON PROFESSIONAL CAREER ...................... 54

44. What software packages are you familiar with? . 54

45. On a scale of 1 to 10, how would you rate yourself as a leader? .............................................................................. 55

46. Are you open to take risks? or Do you like experimenting? ....................................................................... 56

47. What are your future goals? Tell me about your short term and long-term goals. ................................................. 57

48. Why do you want to change job? ........................ 57

49. What do you know about our company? ............ 59

50. What do you like about our company? .............. 60

51. Where do you see yourself in 5 years? ................ 62

52. What's your salary expectation? ........................... 63

53. If we were to celebrate our first year in the company, what would be the greatest result we could celebrate? ...... 64

54. Have you done other job interviews? ................... 64

55. What are your professional aspirations? ............... 65

V

56. Are you willing to relocate?......................................... 67

57. What do you think your tasks will be?..................... 70

58. How did you find this job? ...................................... 71

59. Are You Willing To Travel For The Job? ................. 71

60. Discuss your resume............................................. 74

61. Explain a gap in your employment? ....................... 75

62. If you were to create a company what will be the 3 core values.................................................................... 76

63. If you were to create a company what will be the motto   77

64. Tell me about a time at work when your integrity was challenged. How did you handle it? ............................ 78

HYPOTHETICAL QUESTIONS .......................................... 79

65. How would you handle it if the priorities for a project you were working on were suddenly changed? .................. 80

66. What would you do if you disagreed with the way a manager wanted you to handle a problem? ....................... 81

67. Who are your references? ........................................ 82

68. What would your references say about you?...... 83

69. How would you handle working closely with a colleague who was very different from you? ...................... 86

70. How would you handle an instance of receiving criticism from a superior?................................................. 87

71. Tell me about a time you reached a big goal at work. How did you reach it? ......................................................... 88

72. What would you do if you worked hard on a solution to a problem, and your solution was criticized by your team? 89

NON-CONVENTIONAL QUESTIONS ............................... 91

73. If you were an animal, what would it be? ............... 91

74. How would you fire an employee? ......................... 93

75. If you could start a business, what would you do? 94

76. If someone wrote a biography about you, what would the title be? ................................................................... 96

77. If you were a survivor on a deserted island, what one person would you like to have with you? ........................... 97

78. Which superhero could defeat any other superhero? 98

79. Sell me this pen ....................................................... 99

80. Tell Me a Story. ................................................... 101

PUZZLE AND LOGIC QUESTIONS .................................. 101

81. PUZZLE AND LOGIC QUESTION#1 .................... 101

82. PUZZLE AND LOGIC QUESTION#2 ................. 102

83. PUZZLE AND LOGIC QUESTION#3 ................. 102

84. PUZZLE AND LOGIC QUESTION#4 ................. 103

| | | |
|---|---|---|
| 85. | PUZZLE AND LOGIC QUESTION #5 | 103 |
| 86. | PUZZLE AND LOGIC QUESTION #6 | 104 |
| 87. | PUZZLE AND LOGIC QUESTION #7 | 104 |
| 88. | PUZZLE AND LOGIC QUESTION #8 | 105 |
| 91. | PUZZLE AND LOGIC QUESTION #11 | 106 |
| 92. | PUZZLE AND LOGIC QUESTION #12 | 107 |
| 93. | PUZZLE AND LOGIC QUESTION #13 | 108 |
| 94. | PUZZLE AND LOGIC QUESTION #14 | 109 |
| 95. | PUZZLE AND LOGIC QUESTION #15 | 109 |
| 96. | PUZZLE AND LOGIC QUESTION #16 | 110 |
| 97. | PUZZLE AND LOGIC QUESTION #17 | 111 |
| 98. | PUZZLE AND LOGIC QUESTION #18 | 111 |
| 99. | PUZZLE AND LOGIC QUESTION #19 | 112 |

FINAL QUESTION ............................................................ 115

100. DO YOU HAVE ANY QUESTION FOR ME? .... 115

**THINGS YOU SHOULD NEVER SAY IN A JOB INTERVIEW** ................................................................. 117

"Tell Me What You Do Around Here" ........................... 117

"I Didn't Get Along With My Boss" ............................... 118

"I'm Really Nervous" ..................................................... 118

"I'll Do Whatever" ......................................................... 118

"I Know I Don't Have Much Experience, But…" .......... 119

"Perfectionism Is My Greatest Weakness" ....................... 119

"It's on My Resume" ................................................................ 119

"I Think Outside the Box" ..................................................... 120

"I'd Like to Start My Own Business as Soon as Possible" ................................................................................................. 120

"How Much Vacation Time Do I Get?" ............................. 120

"I Know I Don't Have Much Experience, But…" .......... 121

"Yes! I Have a Great Answer for That!" ........................... 121

"How Soon Do You Promote Employees?" ..................... 122

"Sorry, I'm So Late." ............................................................... 122

HOW TO APPEAR CONFIDENT IN AN INTERVIEW ....... 123

Make eye contact ..................................................................... 124

Maintain good posture .......................................................... 124

Practice your handshake ...................................................... 125

Practice breathing techniques ........................................... 125

Calm your fidgeting ................................................................ 126

Prepare and rehearse your answers ................................ 126

Talk slowly ................................................................................. 127

Dress the part ........................................................................... 127

Think positively ....................................................................... 128

CONCLUSION .................................................................... 129

# MEANING OF INTERVIEW

The word interview comes from Latin, and middle French words meaning to "see between' or "see each other." Generally, an interview means a private meeting between people when questions are asked and answered. The person who answers the questions of an interview is called in the interviewer. The person who asks the questions of our interview is called an interviewer. It suggests a meeting between two persons for the purpose of getting a view of each other or for knowing each other. When we normally think of an interview, we think a setting in which an employer tries to size up an applicant for a job. So, an interview is formal meetings between two people (the interviewer and the interviewee) where questions are asked by the interviewer to obtain information, qualities, attitudes, wishes, etc.

# TYPES OF INTERVIEWS

## BASED ON THE COUNT OF PEOPLE INVOLVED

### One-to-one interview (Personal interview):

It is the most well-known among the interview types; it includes the interviewer posing inquiries perhaps both specialized and general, to the interviewee to examine how to fit the competitor is for the job.

**Example**: Posts in small organizations and mid-level and high-level jobs in big organizations.

### Group interview:

This involves multiple candidates, and they are given a topic for discussion. They are assessed on their conversational ability and how satisfactorily they are able to have their own views and make others believe in them. Here, the best among the lot gets selected.

**Example**: Fresher posts and mid-level sales posts.

## Panel interview (Committee Interview):

The interviewers here are group fr.om among the company people who are in a senior position, and usually, the panel interview is when the candidate is supposed to make a presentation. But many-a-times it could be for the job interview as well.

**Example**: Mid-level and high-level jobs.

# BASED ON THE PLANNING INVOLVED

## A structured interview (Formal interview or guided interview):

Here in the traditional form of an interview, the questions asked are all in a standard format, and the same is used for all the candidates. This is to assess the ability of all the candidates impartially.

**Example**: Entry-level jobs for fresher.

## Unstructured interview (Informal interview or conversational interview):

This is the opposite of a structured interview. Here the interviewer has a definite idea in mind about the questions to be asked, but it doesn't follow a certain format. The interviewer may deviate, and a conversation type interview follows.

**Example**: Mid-level job interview for a managerial position

# BASED ON JUDGING THE ABILITIES;

## Behavioral-based interview:

The interviewee is asked questions about past work experiences and how it was dealt with in a particular situation. This helps the interviewer understand the candidate's future performance based on his past experiences. Here the candidates need to provide examples when they have handled situations. The probing may be in detail to assess the candidate's behavior and responses, and this determines the candidate's future job prospects.

**Example**: Interview for managerial positions, executive posts.

## Problem-solving interview (Task-Oriented interview):

Here the interviewer is more concerned about the problem-solving abilities, be it technical, managerial, creative or analytical skills. This is the most common among the interview patterns, and it may involve either writing and answering a questionnaire set or answering the technical questions orally.

**Example**: Interviews for Software recruitments, technical industries, and managerial positions.

## Depth interview (In-depth interview):

When you need to ascertain everything about the interviewee right from life history, academic qualifications, work experiences, hobbies, and interests, you conduct the depth interview.

Here the interviewer has a clear idea about the questions he will be asking, but once the question is asked, he allows the conversation to flow and is more of a listener. This interview takes time and more of a friendly approach of the interviewer towards the interviewee.

**Example**: For executive posts.

## Stress interview:

Very rare, but such interviews are conducted to see how the candidate will be able to react in stressful situations and to assess if he will be able to handle the crisis at his job.

The tactics involved include:

- Completely ignore the candidate by maybe, making a phone call in the middle of the interview.
- Or some other tactic like continuously interrupting the candidate when he answers the questions.
- Trying to enforce your point of view forcefully even if he disagrees.
- Asking a whole lot of questions all at once.
- Interrupting him by asking another question not related to his answer.

**Example**: For banker jobs.

# BASED ON THE TASK

## Apprenticeship interview:

Here the candidate is a novice, and the interview is a very formal one with general questions and some skill related questions being asked.

**Example**: Interview for training programs in organizations.

## Evaluation interview:

In this interview, a fixed set of questions are asked, and a scoring system evaluates the points scored. This type of interview negates the scope of the personal bias of the interviewer.

**Example**: Interview in corporate organizations

## Promotion interview:

This is for an employee of the company seeking a higher position for career enhancement purposes.

**Example**: Interviews in mid-level posts.

## Counseling interview:

When employees are called, and their problems and solutions are discussed within the organization, such meeting type interviews are called counseling interviews.

**Example**: Interviews in big organizations

## Disciplinary interview:

Here an individual or number of employees or sometimes the employee union is interviewed for their misconduct or non-performance. This is more sort of a meeting between the manager and the employees to get the problem resolved.

**Example**: Interviews in big companies.

## Persuasive interview:

The interviewee here has to persuade the interviewer to accept his point of view as in case of an employee persuading his manager to implement some changes in the policy or a sales manager persisting on selling a product.

**Example**: Interviews in mid-level managerial posts

# OBJECTIVES OF INTERVIEW:

- It helps to verify the information provided by the candidate. It helps to ascertain the accuracy of the provided facts and information about the candidate.
- What the candidate has written in the resume are the main points. What other additional skill set does he have? All these are known by conducting interviews.
- It not only gives the interviewer information about the candidate's technical knowledge but also gives an insight into his much needed creative and analytical skills.
- It helps in establishing a mutual relation between the employee and the company.
- It is useful for the candidate so that he comes to know about his profession, the type of work that is expected from him, and he gets to know about the company.

- It is beneficial for the interviewer and the interviewee as individuals, because both of them gain experience, both professionally and personally.
- It helps the candidate assess his skills and knows where he lacks and the places where he needs improvement.
- It also helps the company build its credentials and image among the employment seeking candidates.

In the current job market, you'd better have your act together, or you won't stand a chance against the competition. Be prepared to the best of your ability. There is no way to predict what an interview holds, but by following these important rules, you will feel less anxious and will be ready to positively present yourself. Check yourself on these basic points before you go on that all-important interview

## Do your research

Researching the company before the interview and learning, however much as could be expected about its administrations, items, clients, and rivalry will give you an edge in comprehension and tending to the company's needs. The more you think about the company and a big motivator for it, the better possibility you have of selling yourself in the interview. You additionally should get some answers concerning the company's way of life to pick up an understanding of your potential satisfaction at work. You ought to have the option to discover a great deal of data about the company's history, crucial qualities, staff, culture, and ongoing victories on its site. On the off chance that the company has a blog and a web-based life nearness, they can be valuable spots to look, as well

## Dress sharp

Try not to hold up until the last moment to choose an interview outfit, print additional duplicates of your resume, or discover a notebook and pen. Have one great interview outfit prepared, so you can interview without prior warning stressing over what to wear. At the point when you have an interview arranged, prepare everything the prior night.

Not exclusively will arranging out everything (from what shoes you will wear, to how you'll style your hair, to what time you will leave and how you'll arrive) get you time toward the beginning of the day, it can help lessen pursuit of employment uneasiness, and it will likewise spare you from deciding, which means you can utilize that intellectual prowess for your interview. Ensure your interview clothing is slick, clean, and fitting for the sort of firm you are interviewing with. Carry a pleasant portfolio with additional duplicates of your resume. Incorporate a pen and paper for note-taking.

# Be punctual

Be on time for the interview. On-time means five to ten minutes early. If need be, drive to the interview location ahead of time, so you know exactly where you are going and how long it will take to get there. Take into account the time of your interview so you can adjust for local traffic patterns at that time. Give yourself a few extra minutes to visit the restroom, check your outfit, and calm your nerves.

# Make your selling points clear

If a tree falls in the forest and no one is there to hear it, did it make a sound? More important, if you communicate your selling points during a job interview and the interviewer doesn't get it, did you score? On this question, the answer is clear: No! So don't bury your selling points in long-winded stories. Instead, tell the interviewer what your selling point is first, then give the example.

# Speak the right body language

Dress appropriately, make eye contact, give a firm handshake, have good posture, speak clearly, and don't wear perfume or cologne! Sometimes interview locations are small rooms that may lack good air circulation. You want the interviewer paying attention to your job qualifications -- not passing out because you've come in wearing Malizia and the candidate before you were doused with Brut, and the two have mixed to form a poisonous gas that results in you not getting an offer.

# Be Succinct (and Definitely, Don't Recite Your Resume)

Whatever you do, don't waste this time regurgitating every single detail of your career. Most people answer it like they're giving a dissertation on their resume, but that's only going to bore the interviewer to tears.

There's no deductively demonstrated ideal length for noting this or any interview question. A few mentors and spotters will guide you to hold it to 30 seconds or less, while others will say you should go for a moment, or talk for close to two minutes. Be that as it may, in his experience, individuals will in general, start losing steam after 1.5 to 2.5 minutes of continuous talking. You'll need to choose what feels directly for you in some random setting, yet in case you're representing longer than a few minutes, there's a decent possibility you're diving into an excess of detail too early. Ensure you're additionally perusing the room as you're talking. In the event that the other individual looks exhausted or diverted, it may be an ideal opportunity to wrap it up. On the off chance that they liven up at one piece of your answer, it may merit developing that point more.

# Follow-Up After the Interview

Always follow up with a thank-you note reiterating your interest in the position. You can also include any details you may have forgotten to mention during your interview. If you interview with multiple people from the same company, send each one a personal note. Send your thank-you email within 24 hours of your interview.

# THE TOP 100 COMMON QUESTIONS

## FIVE MOST COMMON QUESTIONS

### 1. Tell me about yourself

Often asked at the very start of an interview, this is your opportunity to deliver an elevator pitch that gives the interviewer a quick idea of who you are. Used wisely, this elevator pitch could make the interviewer very interested in your next answer. Used incorrectly, the interviewer could stop paying attention before you even have a chance to answer a second question.

**Example**: "Currently, I serve as the assistant to three of the company's five executive team members, including the CEO. From my 12 years of experience as an official collaborator, I've built up the capacity to envision barriers and make compelling elective plans. My most prominent incentive to any official is my capacity to work autonomously, saving their opportunity to concentrate on the requirements of the business. Plainly you're searching for somebody who comprehends the subtleties of dealing with a CEO's bustling day and can proactively handle issues. As somebody with an eye for detail and a drive to arrange, I blossom with ensuring each day has an unmistakable arrangement, and each arrangement is obviously imparted."

## 2. Describe yourself

When an interviewer asks you to talk about yourself, they're looking for information about how your qualities and characteristics align with the skills they believe are required to succeed in the role. If possible, include quantifiable results to demonstrate how you use your best attributes to drive success.

**Example:** "I would say that as a security officer, I'm vigilant, proactive, and committed to ensuring safe, secure, and orderly environments. In my last incident response rating, I received a 99% against the team average, which has been at around 97% over the past 3 years. I like to be thorough, documenting all incidents. I'm also a lifelong learner, always seeking out the latest security equipment and techniques to patrol buildings. I frequently make suggestions to management about security improvements and changes as my motivation comes from making a meaningful contribution."

## 3. Why should we choose you?

While this question may seem like an intimidation tactic, interviewers generally bring this up to offer you another opportunity to explain why you're the best candidate. Your answer should address the skills and experience you offer and why you're a good culture fit.

**Example:** "I have a passion for application development that's grown stronger over the course of my career. The company's mission aligns with my personal values, and, from my limited time in the office, I can already tell this is the sort of positive culture in which I would thrive. I want to work for a company that has the potential to reshape the industry, and I believe you're doing just that."

## 4. What are your strengths?

Don't choose something irrelevant to the job or the employer, like your skill in Sudoku (unless Sudoku expertise is a requirement for this job). You have many strengths, but pick the one they need help with the most. Is it your expertise in a particular skill or technology? Is it your ability to turn low-performing teams into high performers? Share something that makes them think they need to hire you.

**Example:** "I'm a natural problem-solver. I find it rewarding to dig deep and uncover solutions to challenges—it's like solving a puzzle. It's something I've always excelled at, and something I enjoy. Much of product development is about finding innovative solutions to challenging issues, which is what drew me to this career path in the first place."

## 5. What are your weaknesses?

It can feel unbalanced to examine your weaknesses in a domain where you're relied upon to concentrate on your achievements. Notwithstanding, when addressed effectively, sharing your weaknesses can show that you are mindful and need to ceaselessly improve at your specific employment—attributes that are amazingly appealing to numerous businesses. Make sure, to begin with, the weakness and afterward talk about the measures you've taken to improve. Along these lines, you're completing your answer on a positive note. You can likewise share instances of aptitudes you have improved, giving explicit examples of how you have perceived weakness and found a way to address it.

**Example:** "My most noteworthy weakness used to be tarrying. Companions who realized my work style would prod me, saying, "Frenzy hastens execution." In school, I was the individual who destroyed dusk 'til dawn affairs to complete their article directly before the cutoff time. This isn't as flippant as it sounds from the minute I'm relegated an undertaking, I'm contemplating it. A large portion of my first and second drafts get created rationally, so it's just a matter of recording the last draft. What's more, since I have an amazing direction of language, I don't need to invest a lot of energy editing or reconsidering." However, after I found my first employment as a substance essayist, it turned out to be certain that while this procedure worked for me (I've never missed a cutoff time), it made my editorial manager incredibly anxious. Thus I've figured out how to set "early" cutoff times for myself in any event 24 hours before the genuine cutoff time, so my activities currently consistently land with a lot of time to save.

## QUESTIONS ON YOUR PERSON

### 6. What is your dream?

This question is designed to find out if you're going to stick around or move on as soon as you find a better opportunity. Keep your answer focused on the job and the company, and reiterate to the interviewer that the position aligns with your long-term goals. Additionally, this question is used to gauge your ambition, expectations for your career, and your ability to plan ahead. The best way to handle this question is to determine your current career trajectory and how this role plays in helping you reach your ultimate goals.

**Example:** "I would like to continue developing my marketing expertise as well as my leadership skills over the next several years. One of the reasons I'm interested in working for a fast-growing start-up company is that I'll have the ability to wear many hats and collaborate with many different departments. I believe this experience will serve me well in achieving my ultimate goal of someday leading a marketing department."

## 7. How do you relieve stress?

Many jobs are stressful or have stressful components to them. Employers want to know how you'll handle yourself when times get tough. Do you outwardly explode, get quiet and withdraw, or feel motivated to push through? While you want to be honest, take a more positive approach to your answer:

**Example:** "When I get stressed out, I find it's best for me to take a step back and make a plan of attack. This helps me get a handle on the situation and figure out what I need to do to alleviate my stress and get things accomplished."

## 8. How would you feel about having a younger boss?

This can be a very awkward question, so the most important approach is to remain positive. If nothing else, this will communicate your ability to remain focused on unusual circumstances, your interviewer will learn about your ability to follow instructions. Even if your manager is not younger than you, it will be beneficial to know you are willing to take orders regardless of any unusual situation.

**Example:** The thought of whether I am reporting to a younger or older person never enters my mind. My superiors are my superiors. Age never enters into that. Likewise, no other quality or personal attribute will affect my ability to follow instructions.

## 9. Among the personal interests, you have the reading: what is the last book you have read?

You have to stay away from anything that makes you look unprofessional. Don't mention books that fall in the following genres: Fantasy, Science, Fiction, Fan Fiction, Cheesy Romance, Pop Mystery (Dean Koontz), Self Help, Vampires/Teen Books Made Into Movies, etc. Non-fiction, classics, standard fiction, poetry, essay writing and some of the more well-written mystery novels are all fair game. Be ready to explain the book in its entirety because if the employer has read the book they are going to want to talk about it with you to ensure you are not making it up. Remember, what you read says a lot about who you are. You want the employer to think that you are a brilliant and educated individual, and your guilty pleasures (like romance novels) should be kept out of the workplace.

**Example:** "Unfortunately, I have not had the opportunity to read for pleasure in quite some time. However, I have been brushing up on some basic sales books. I recently completed 'Close Like the Pros' by Steve Marx and 'Take the Cold Out of Cold

Calling' by Sam Richter. I have also recently completed 'Presentation Zen' by Garr Reynolds. Once I have finished brushing up on sales techniques, though, I hope to start 'The Journey or' by Gary Jennings."

I think it is a question just to see if you are a well-rounded person. But, you could also use the question as an opportunity to demonstrate something unique about you or to bring up an aspect of yourself not previously addressed.

## 10. Which is your favorite book

If you haven't read a book in years, just find a short book about something that interests you. Be relatively familiar with the book, but it is very unlikely you will be asked about a specific passage. Just have something to say about it and why it interests you.

## 11. How do you evaluate success?

Think deeper about what the interview question you are asked really means. There is usually some hidden meaning that they are trying to get to. If you are able to understand this hidden meaning, your answer can focus on it specifically, which strengthens your answer.

The question, "How do you determine or evaluate success has some hidden meaning. You should not focus on your definition of success, but rather how your definition shapes your work ethic. The interviewer is interested in what qualities will allow you to succeed. They want to be confident that you are self-motivated and dedicated to your work.

*Points to Emphasize*

- Figure out which qualities they are trying to find in you and focus on them. These may vary with the specific job, but they should be, more or less, consistent.
- Even though you are focusing on your attributes, remember to answer the question. Start by defining success.
- You should probably include going above expectations in your answer. This is the most common goal for this question. Do you consider yourself successful when you meet the minimum expectations or when you do the job, right?
- If you are interviewing for a management position, their expectations for your answer may be different. Instead, you might focus on what your expectations for employees under you are.
- Be confident without being prideful.

**Example:** I determine success as getting the job done properly. Even if the expectations are lower, I will not consider myself successful unless I met all of my own personal requirements. Of course, I'm always trying to push my personal requirements higher and higher. I welcome opportunities to improve.

## 12. What are the characteristics of a good boss, according to you?

As a major aspect of the interview procedure, employers should survey how you'll react to supervision in case you're procured. They'll attempt to decide if you have any issues with power, so your interviewer may pose inquiries about your favored boss trying to make sense of how well you'll function inside the organization's administration framework. Whether you've had incredible past encounters with bosses or they were an aggregate bad dream, addressing this inquiry can, in fact, be similar to navigating a precarious situation. It can have a firm arrangement going in for what you'll need to state and not say.

You'll need to underline your capacity to work freely just as your solace with taking heading from a boss. You would prefer not to appear to be requiring excessively or too little supervision. Consider the activity you're interviewing for before you answer, and attempt to evaluate how a lot of the board the employer will expect that you'll require. Utilize this to direct your answer

**Example**: "My perfect boss would support clear correspondence among herself and her workers. I accept that correspondence—face to face, just as by means of telephone and email—is basic to a fruitful connection between an employer and worker.

## 13. What do you do in your spare time?

Not all the questions you get asked in an interview pertaining to the job. Sometimes a recruiter or hiring manager wants to get to know what you're interested in outside of a work environment, in order to get a feel for what you're like as a person (and not just a potential employee). The answer to the question "What do you do in your spare time?" is meant to shed light on your personality, and provide a little insight into how you might gel with others in an office. When you're asked this question in a job interview, the interviewer is not usually looking for a specific "right answer" (although many wrongs do answers exist; more about that below). Your goal when answering should be to share information that provides the employer with an accurate sense of who you are without disclosing something that might disqualify you for the job. Remember that you may need to "live with" the answer you provide if you receive and accept a job offer. So, keep in mind the expectations you are creating yourself as a potential employee when formulating your response. When you answer this question, you want to talk about hobbies or activities that will cast you in a positive light. Answer in a way that demonstrates your personality, intelligence, and range of interests.

Talk about hobbies that keep you physically active—it shows that you take your health seriously, which is always a good thing. Bring up any volunteer work that you do. This shows that you have concern for others besides yourself, and says a lot about your integrity and character. Mention activities that better you for the job, like attending seminars or conferences, reading fiction or non-fiction, or learning new languages. This shows you have a desire to learn new things and stay on top of your game.

**Example:** In my spare time, I enjoy riding horses. Horses have always been a part of my life, and right now I'm learning dressage, which is very challenging. I also lead a trail riding group for other horse lovers once a month.

## 14. How do you like working?

This question helps interviewers decide whether you will fit in well with the company culture and the requirements of the job. For instance, if you require complete silence and focus to work, but the office has a bustling, collaborative atmosphere (and an open floor plan), you might not be a strong fit. When answering this question, it is important to keep a particular job in mind. Avoid clichés (like "hard worker" and "good communication skills") and focus on specific elements of your work style that fit with the position and company. This question is far easier to answer if you do some research before the job interview. Analyze the job listing to match your qualifications with their requirements, and prepare answers that show how your work style makes you the best candidate for the job. It's also important to be honest while still highlighting the positive. Don't claim to be a perfectionist if you're a big-picture person; instead, emphasize your vision and commitment to quality.

**Example:** My work style is extremely flexible—working on so many different projects requires me to be adaptive. In general, I try to work on one project at a time, working as quickly, but efficiently, as possible to achieve the best results. All of my projects require collaboration, so I use the team environment to check for errors. I am a perfectionist and a driven worker, and I think my clear communication skills allow me to bring out the best in any team, in any project.

## 15. Describe to me a situation in which you put your skills into practice!

It's about finding out whether you and your skills are a good match for the position. In fact, that's one of the main reasons an employer invites you to an interview. You'll need to describe situations that demonstrate your:

work-specific or technical skills. These include using a software program, repairing a piece of equipment, or teaching a class.

Employability or transferable skills. For example, the personal, teamwork, and fundamental skills you need to succeed in every work situation.

**Example:** As an expert in relations, my education began learning the basics of communication. This proved to be the foundation for my entire education. As I advanced, I would come back to the interpersonal relations knowledge that I acquired. In particular, I remember a project we had that required us to go out and interact with members of different cultures in different ways. I was only able to complete the assignment because of the skills I had already developed. In fact, I am still putting these foundational skills into practice now that I have entered the working world and am working toward advancing in my career.

## 16. Do you work well under stress?

Employers know that everyone feels stressed at one point or the other while performing their task. So when you are asked interview questions about how you deal with stress, the interviewer does not expect you say that you don't feel stressed. The interviewer only wants to know how stress affects you and how you go about dealing with it. When you are answering this question, you pay attention to the following:

- Give an example of how you have handled stress well in the past
- Talk about a stressful situation that is related to the work
- Walk the interview through how you managed stress previously

**Example:** "I know that sometimes it is hard to avoid stress, but I try to face the situation, rather than being stressed. Regardless of how much work I have to do, I make sure that I tackle the situation rather than being overwhelmed by the problem. That way, I handle the situation better and don't get stressed. For example, when I dealt with an unsatisfied customer that was really angry and was ready to give a negative review about our product. Instead of feeling stressed, I concentrated on finding out what her challenge was exactly and looked for ways to help her get the problem solved, addressing it to the right channel. My ability to remain calm when dealing with the unsatisfied customer reduced my stress and the stress that the customer may face".

## 17. How do you work in a team?

Most jobs, at least those in traditional work settings – require that you be able to communicate and work well with others. Try to provide a recent example or two of how you've contributed to a team at your job.

**Example**: I prefer to work as a team member because I believe that the best ideas are developed in partnership with others. I'm equally comfortable being a team member and a team lead, a few months ago I was selected to lead our team in a deadline-critical implementation project. Because of our great teamwork, we were able to produce our deliverables to the client well before the deadline.

## 18. Do you prefer to work alone or in a team?

Most employers and hiring managers know that communication is one thing that can make a business thrive. So interviewers may ask you this question to discover how well you can work in a team. If you lack good communication skills, then you cannot thrive in a team. As a job-seeker, you should make use of this opportunity to tell the interviewer that you are a good team player. When you are answering this question, you should take note of the following:

Emphasize your sociability and ability to work alone

Give an example of an experience that showcases how well you can interact with others effectively

Make sure that your response is related to the position that you are applying for, you should also avoid giving the impression that you don't need to interact with others and also being judgmental about other people.

**Example:** I am equally comfortable in either situation, actually. In my last job, I had the opportunity to do both independent and team projects, and I really enjoyed the variety. My favorite work scenario is when we begin a project as a team, brainstorming our approaches and establishing our deadlines and individual responsibilities before going off to work independently on our assigned tasks. Even when working independently, however, I think it's invaluable to be able to reach out to a team for advice and support. I also make sure that I'm available to help other project team members when they need assistance.

### 19. Which role do you play in a team?

Some people are natural leaders, while others are excellent followers. By asking this question, an employer is trying to gauge both how you would fit into the department's current team dynamics and to assess whether you are someone they should flag for eventual leadership responsibilities.

**Example:** While I'm happy being a strong team player, I also love being able sometimes to take the lead and coordinate everyone's efforts. I have great organizational, scheduling, and follow-up skills, which is why my supervisor and other team members often call upon me to take the lead on important projects, such as our major new mobile technology system acquisition last year.

### 20. If you asked your friends to describe you, what is the adjective I would hear most often?

*Tips for What to Say*

- Highlight one personality trait at a time, sharing an example of a time when you demonstrated this quality.

Storytelling is an opportunity to display confidence, charisma, and strong interpersonal skills.
- Focus on the personality traits that apply to the job for which you are applying. Of course, be positive, but make sure you are honest and humble also, as these virtues are highly valued in the workforce. Moreover, embellishing your assets or flat-out lying could land you in a company culture that is incompatible with your true nature.

## 21. Which person is a source of inspiration for you?

By the interview stage, you should have a good understanding of the role you have applied for and be able to identify what it is the employer is looking for, It's important to get across that your skills, experience, and personality match the role. If you've done your research and you have a good grasp of the employer's mission, then you'll find it easier to match your motivations with the role.

Consider the role that you are applying for and which areas genuinely provide you with job satisfaction. This should help you understand and craft the best answer

For example, if the employer is seeking a 'self-starter who thrives in a target-driven environment,' it's essential you talk about how you are motivated by targets and love the freedom of being able to use your initiative to deliver results. Prepare some examples that center around how you derive job satisfaction.

Prepare high-energy stories, which capture roles that have motivated you in the past. If your style is naturally quiet and downbeat, rehearse replies that have more uplift, A good approach is to describe the goals you'd target in the role you're interviewing for. The same goes for questions like:" What would an excellent performance look like in this role? "What would you do in the first month of the job?"

## 22. Tell me about something not on your resume.

Your resume states the facts, but the interviewer wants to know about the person behind the work history. This will help your interviewer determine whether you're a good match for the job and the organization.

There are several different ways you can answer the question. Share a strength that isn't on your resume or Share an intangible strength.

For example, public speaking might be an important requirement in the job for which you're being considered. You may not have had the opportunity to speak in front of groups during your work history. However, you could respond that you were on the debate team in college, excelled at presentations as part of group projects in school, gave a talk at a volunteer dinner, or won a marketing competition as an undergraduate. Or perhaps you want to emphasize your commitment, willingness to go the extra mile, and creative problem-solving skills.

## 23. What is your favorite quote?

Quotes can be quite powerful. What you interpret a quote to mean can be quite different from what someone else thinks it means. Be careful to select something that is not too revealing personally or shows a leaning towards controversial opinions. If possible, select something about leadership or a strong work ethic. Explain why you selected it and what it means to you.

**Sample answer:** I heard this one as a teenager when I was still trying to figure out what I wanted to be. It is a quote by Bruce Springsteen, "My parents always told me to get a little something for myself. What they didn't know was, was that I wanted everything". It inspired me to reach higher for my goals and not to settle. I knew that it wouldn't be easy, but if I maintained a strong work ethic, I could achieve what I wanted.

## 24. What is your spiritual practice?

This falls into the region of questions that a prospective employer should never actually ask, especially in Australia, because seeking details that could be used as the basis of discrimination, including religious affiliation, is contrary to anti-discrimination law.

There is a very narrow and specific set of circumstances where it is an allowable question, such as religious bodies employing those to take part in religious observances, but for the most part, employers aren't allowed to ask questions that could give the appearance of potential discrimination in interviews.

## 25. What do you do to improve yourself?

Questions about self-improvement or areas of biggest weakness are extremely common in job interviews. They are so common that they play a role at almost every interview in some form, so you really need to be prepared to answer. The question can be asked a number of different ways, in addition to what would you like to improve yourself? The key to answering this question is to either talk about what you're learning or turning it back on the interviewer. The interviewer wants to know that you plan to improve it, whatever it may be.

Improving yourself also does not just have to be about a weakness. It can also be about strength. If you want, you can provide an answer similar to how you would answer a question about your greatest weakness. However, you are being asked about where you would like to improve, not what you are worst at. So you may also want to give an answer about how you would like to improve many things.

**Example answer:** "I would like to improve in every facet of my life. No matter how much I may excel at a particular skill or task, I believe I can always get better and would like an opportunity to gain new experiences that will help me become better at anything I undertake. Does your company offer any extended training courses that I can take advantage of?"

# QUESTIONS AND SKILLS AND EXPERIENCE

## 26. Tell me about your past experiences

It is no news that employers look forward to hiring candidates that have the right kind of experience that would help them perform the job well. When interviewers ask you this question, they want to know how your experience will help you perform the job better than other candidates.

The interviewer also wants to know how your experience aligns with the description of the job that you are applying for. Hiring managers judge your experience to see if you are going to add value to the position that you are interviewing for.

You should take note of the following when you are answering this question:

- Describe your experience in your previous job and how it relates to the job that you are applying for

- You can also talk about your achievements in your previous jobs that will be useful in the position that you are applying for
- It is important for you to be honest about your job experience

**Example:** I developed great skills like problem-solving and patience, assisting customers with our product even when they are really frustrated. I am excellent at enduring customer's rage and finding a way to help them solve their problems and make them become satisfied customers. During my stay in my previous company, our returning customer rate rose from 2 to 10% that year. Since improving customer satisfaction is the major goal in this role, I know that my experience in customer service will be of great value to this company"

## 27. What are your greatest successes?

The interviewer is giving you the opportunity to choose a story you want to highlight in the interview. You're not being limited to talking about teamwork or leadership or even necessarily a work accomplishment. This puts some power in your hands to influence how the interviewer sees you, so you want to be prepared. The example that you choose will say a lot about you. First, it will give clues about what you value most. Were you most proud of closing a huge deal or building a great team? This will help indicate if you're a good fit for the job and the culture.

Your answer will also help them envision you at your best. This is why it's important not to choose an underwhelming example and to prepare how you tell the story to make sure you emphasize your best thinking and contributions

## 28. What kind of qualifications do you have?

Stop and think for a moment before responding to a question like, "What qualifications do you have?" You need to respond succinctly and clearly, and you need to stick to the question. So don't rattle off everything that is in your repertoire, and don't try to present yourself as a Jack-of-all-trades. To do this, you could quote former managers, colleagues, or vendors. Another compelling way to back up your claims is to quantify an achievement.

**For example:** In my previous role, I was tasked with growing new product revenue by six percent. I exceeded that goal and grew my product revenue by a CAGR of eight percent.

## 29. Why didn't you work this year?

It's beyond infuriating that as a job-seeker, qualified and ready to work, you have to worry about answering the question, "Why aren't you working right now?" as though being unemployed were a crime. You can even start to feel vaguely guilty as you sit in the interview chair, although you haven't done anything wrong.

**Sample answer**: "It was clear that it was time for me to leave my last job and I really wanted to focus on my job search, versus trying to juggle my job search with a very demanding full-time job. So, I left the job to become a full-time job-seeker and find my next opportunity."

## 30. I see you have no experience in the [any] field?

If you feel like you've got transferrable experience that the interviewer maybe isn't factoring in, start by asking questions. Inquire about that organization's biggest challenges, top goals, and immediate priorities for the person they hire. Be genuine and curious. And then, if appropriate, present your background or ideas in a way that doesn't make people feel like you're ripping on how they operate. Instead, it gently leads them to that spot at which they can see how your tangential or complementary background may be of genuine value to the overall organization.

## 31. What did you do when you disagreed with your superiors?

When you get asked about a time when you disagreed with your boss, the interviewer is really asking about your communication skills. Disagreements happen. What you do when those disagreements take place says a lot about you. The hiring manager is looking to see that you have a good relationship with those in authority. How you interact with your previous boss also says a lot about you as a person. The interviewer uses questions like these to see if you'll be a good fit in the company.

*Points to Emphasize*

When you answer this question, you want to focus on traits, skills, and experiences that helped you diffuse the disagreement.

- Talk about how this situation with your boss will prepare you to handle disagreements with co-workers in the future.
- Mention that your laid back personality trait will help diffuse tension.
- Briefly explain the situation of the disagreement, but make sure to do so in a respectful way. Don't be afraid to admit that you were in the wrong if that's what happened.
- Talk about the importance of communicating with co-workers even if there is a disagreement

## 32. Tell me the last mistake you made

Although no one likes talking about their mistakes, being able to discuss your past mistakes in a job interview can actually be a great way of impressing the interviewer. So when you encounter a question like, "Tell me about a time you made a mistake," during an interview, you should focus on how you dealt with the mistake and what you were able to learn from it. When the hiring manager asks this question, it's not because they're trying to trip you up;

rather, it's a chance for the interviewer to see that you are able to acknowledge your mistakes and learn from them, two very important qualities. An employer would rather hire candidates who admit and grow from their mistakes than those who think they never make any.

**Sample answer:** "At my previous internship, I underestimated the amount of time I would need to work on a presentation for a team meeting. I was still getting used to the workflow in a busy office, so I didn't realize that I would need an extra few hours to put a deck together. Luckily, I managed to catch the mistake before the presentation was due to take place and asked my manager for help to complete it in time. It was a valuable lesson in time management, and I've become better at prioritization and mapping out my schedule as a result of that experience."

## 33. Why have you been fired?

Be very careful with this question. It sounds like an invitation to complain about your previous employer. Interviews are a bad time to trash anyone, even the previous employer who eliminated your job.

Let the interviewer decide on their own if they care about how badly management performed. Just make a simple statement about the cause of the layoff (as it was explained to you upon exit), and then quickly follow with a question about the stability of their company and history with layoffs.

## 34. Have you had any volunteering experience?

Ideally, you are involved in non-work volunteer activities that are related either directly or indirectly, to your career. This can include involvement in professional associations related to your career or any type of volunteer outreach related to your career. If you do not have a career-related volunteer activity, it is acceptable to talk about other volunteer activities as long as they do not show a political or religious affiliation. If you have no outside volunteer activities, just answer the question truthfully: "At this point in my life, I don't have any volunteer activities outside of work, due to my full-time dedication to my work." You can expand this answer by asking if they would be interested in past volunteer activities and/or plans for future volunteer activities.

**Sample answer**: "Yes, I've been involved with our local industry association over the past several years. I started getting more active by assisting with the planning for the annual meeting; then, in the past two years, I've been elected to leadership positions on the Board, first as Treasurer and this year as Vice-President. We just had the elections for next year, and I was recently voted the President-elect, so I will be starting my role as President at the beginning of next year…"

# 35. Have you built long-lasting friendships in your previous jobs?

Although you shouldn't lie about your relationship with your previous job, you should always speak positively about your boss and the relationship you had. We all know that not every boss is a good one. In fact, there are plenty of aggressive, unqualified bosses out there who make working with them extremely unpleasant. That being said, if you badmouth a former boss, it gives you a negative image and the hiring manager will perceive you as a person who doesn't get along well with others, or who may give their own company a bad reputation if they hire you and you don't get along with your boss there. This question is meant to show employers how you are to work with, more than how your previous bosses were to work with.

*Tips:*

- Never badmouth or go into details about negative behavior from a previous boss.
- Focus the question of showing the hiring manager what a good person you are to work with, and how well you get along with others.
- Even if your relationship with your boss was a bad one, talk about what you did to try to improve the relationship and communication.

## 36. Aren't you too qualified for this role?

Interviewers will frequently ask applicants if they feel they are overqualified for the job for which they are applying. The interviewer is asking this question because they want to make sure the candidate the decide upon will stay in the position and not hop quickly to a job that better suits their experience, skills, and abilities. Answering this question can be difficult if you have not prepared yourself for it in advance.

*Best Answers to "Are You Overqualified for This Job?"*

These examples may help you craft your own answers to this question. Keep in mind that you can customize these answers to fit your particular circumstances and the job you're applying for.

- "Overqualified? Some would say that I'm not overqualified but fully qualified. With due respect, could you explain the problem with someone doing the job better than expected?"
- "Fortunately, I've lived enough years to have developed a judgment that allows me to focus on the future. Before we speak of past years, past titles, and past salaries can we look at my strengths and abilities and how I've stayed on the cutting edge of my career field, including its technology?"
- "I hope you're not concerned that hiring someone with my solid experience and competencies would look like

age bias if, once on the job, you decided you'd made a mistake, and I had to go. Can I present a creative idea? Why don't I work on a trial basis for a month—no strings—which would give you a chance to view me up close? This immediately solves your staffing problem at no risk to you. I can hit the floor running and require less supervision than a less experienced worker. When can I start?"

## 37. Was there a person who made the difference in your career?

When a hiring manager asks who has made a difference in your career, they want to find out what motivates you. Understanding what motivates you will give them a bit of insight into what you find important. Having a mentor also shows that you can work well with others. It also shows humility because you can admit that you didn't get to where you are on your own. When an interviewer asks this question, they want to figure out how you will fit in at their company.

*Points to Emphasize*

There are certain points about your role model that will say a lot about you too.

- Talk about the qualities that led you to them as a leader.

- Describe what they helped you learn and how it made you a better professional.
- Give an idea of where you were before this person made a difference.
- Help the hiring manager understand what traits are important to you in a co-worker.
- Giving the interviewer an idea of who shaped you will show them the type of worker that you are.

## 38. What was the most boring job of your career?

When a hiring manager asks you about your most boring job, they want to find out how goal-oriented you are. If you go into a job, no matter how boring, with a set of goals that you want to achieve, the job may not be that boring to you. The interviewer is also trying to get a sense of how long you tend to stay with jobs. Do you get bored easily and then decide it's time to move on The hiring manager wants to make sure that you will fit in with the company and find the work interesting enough to stay for a long time.

*Points to Emphasize*

When you answer this question, you have to emphasize certain points in order to show the hiring manager that you are dedicated.

- You can talk about the most boring job you've ever had.
- Follow it up with reasons why it wasn't that boring for you like the goals you had set for yourself in that job.
- Talk about the importance of challenging yourself. Express traits you have that make it easy to find enjoyment in even the smallest of tasks.
- Keep this answer positive even though it's supposed to highlight the negative.

**Sample answer:** I have had jobs that lend themselves to being boring. When I was a kid, I had a summer job at a city park, and if you weren't looking for things to do, you could just wait around for customers all day. I could see how that job would be boring, but I never let that happen to me. I think it's important to take the initiative in situations where things are a little slow. There's always something that can be done. Some problems to fix or things to clean. I'm a hard worker, so I never allowed myself to have the downtime that would make a job boring. I always kept goals for myself.

## 39. Why did you choose your field of study?

The interviewer is asking, "Why did you choose your field of study?" to understand how much planning went into your career selection. Are you there in the interview seat completely by chance, or are you there because the job at hand is part of a well-designed plan?

There is no right or wrong way to answer this interview question. What the interviewer wants to get a handle on is how much thought and effort you've put into your career goals. You should use this opportunity to showcase your relevant natural talents, as well as the skills you've learned that would be relevant to the position you're interviewing for. If your field of study doesn't necessarily apply to the position, focus on how what you learned can transfer or apply to the job. An education is invaluable, so if you answer carefully, you will be able to convince the interviewer that your degree will help you fulfill the job responsibilities. You'll need to connect your field of study, and what you've gained educationally, to the job you're interviewing for.

Write down the list of skills and experiences you gained through the process of getting your degree. If you're struggling with that, think of all the assignments and projects you completed in school, what skills did you develop working on those assignments and projects? How many of those skills relate to the requirements of the job? Then, focus on those skills when answering this question in an interview.

**Sample answer:** "I'd always wanted to be a writer, so I thought my school's professional writing program would help me figure out which writing niche would be best for me. I soon discovered that I had a passion for editing and publishing, so I worked in several related internship programs throughout my time at college. Now, I feel fully ready to take my first big step into the professional world of publishing."

## 40. Can you describe a complex problem you had to solve?

This is one of the behavioral interview questions that interviewers ask to know the candidate's problem-solving abilities. Employers understand that challenges are inevitable in any work situation, but they want to understand how you face challenges.

**Sample Answer:** "In my previous role as a secondary school teacher, I discovered that I had a very rude student that was bent on not following any instruction that I give. This got me worried because the boy will not follow any instructions that I give, and because of that he was doing badly in his academics, and the management was worried about his situation. I thought it was a minor case until I noticed that the boy had influenced almost everyone in the class. Almost all the students that I teach no longer listen to me and this made it difficult for me to teach them and for them to even learn. So I decided to call this boy and talk to him instead of going back to the management of this situation. As I spoke to the boy, I discovered that the boy doesn't like the fact that he is a science student, which makes him really angry, so he is trying to discourage every other person from paying attention in the class because he is not interested. Finding out this, I counseled him and spoke to his parents about it. The boy was then moved to the Arts, and that was how I could get my peace back as a teacher".

## 41. What was your most significant accomplishment in your previous job?

Interviewers ask candidates questions about their accomplishments to find out if the candidate is a good fit for the job that he/she is applying for. Answering this question well will help the interviewer get an understanding of your value and interest. Your answer to this question will help the interviewer decide whether your personality will be the best fit for this company. This question also gives the interviewer an idea of the accomplishment that he expects from you if you are given the job.

**Sample answer**: "I had several accomplishments in my previous job, but the most notable one was during my internship when I had to urgently replace a team member in the IT team. The company has been working on a project for over a long time, and while the team had gone halfway, a team member that was handling working on the mobile version for iOS resigned immediately, and due to the urgency of the project, I had to replace him. Due to the fact that I had developed an APP for iOS and no other person in the team could do that, I worked on the project for the remaining 6 months of my internship. I completed the project when my internship was ending. After developing the

APP, the project was launched, and I was applauded for the good work. I was also glad to know that the APP already had over 150 reviews before the end of my internship".

## 42. Do you take any work home if you have not finished it

Employers ask this question for a variety of reasons. They might want to know that you are organized and can do all of your work in the allotted time. They also might want to make sure you maintain a decent work-life balance (which many employers believe will ultimately make you a happier, and thus better, employee). However, some employers really are looking for people who make work at the center of their lives, and want to assess just how dedicated to the job you will be. Even employers who do not expect in-depth work on projects after business hours may want employees to frequently check email from home. For some roles, a certain amount of after-hours work is built-in. For instance, a social media manager for a late-night TV show may have monitor online comments after business hours.

Answering this question, therefore, requires you to know a bit about the particular company and job.

**Sample Answers :** When I need to, bringing work home with me is not a problem. I realize the importance of meeting deadlines and getting work done on time, and sometimes that requires extra hours in the office or at home.

I am extremely organized and skilled at budgeting my time. When I begin a project, I create a timeline for myself that allows me to complete the assignment in a timely manner without taking my work home. However, I understand that sometimes timelines change or issues come up, and I am always willing to take work home with me when that happens.

When I begin a new project, I often choose to take work home with me in order to ensure that I complete the project for my client on time. However, maintaining regular time to spend with my family is very important to me, so I try to limit this to the early stages of projects and to urgent matters. I'm very aware of how speedily communications move in this industry. One email can be the difference between landing a pitch or having it go elsewhere. To that end, I try to be very responsive to email on my phone. I do a quick scan of my inbox several times a night when I'm home and look at my email during my early morning workout, too. I always encourage my team to reach out if anything's urgent. And, for the few times a year when I totally unplug, I prep with a back-up network so that all team members know who to contact for feedback and answers.

## 43. Have built a long-lasting relationship in your previous work

During an interview, contracting supervisors need to get a feeling of who you are past your resume. The most effortless approach to do this is by posing inquiries intended to draw out your character. One of these inquiries is, "have you fabricated an enduring kinship in your past activity?" This is a typical inquiry you may experience during an interview for a temporary job or a section level work. At the point when the interviewer asks this present, this is on the grounds that they need to measure how others see you, how mindful you are and how you work with a group.

There are numerous characteristics that intrigue to employers, including reliability, diligent work, and authority. When choosing what quality to feature, ensure that it's an exact impression of you and that you can back it up with models how it has molded your associations with your friends. Are you the pioneer of the pack? Try not to be hesitant to make reference to this. In case you're the go-to companion for making arrangements and executing them, this is unquestionably something you need to feature to your future employer. Accentuate the authority aptitudes you have and your encounters with being a pioneer.

# QUESTIONS ON PROFESSIONAL CAREER

## 44. What software packages are you familiar with?

Make sure you know each of your skills thoroughly. In case you don't know a particular software package or terminology, please do not talk about it in front of the interviewer.

**Sample Answers**

- I am proficient in Operating Systems like Windows and Linux. I am familiar with Microsoft Word, Excel, and PowerPoint from the Microsoft Office Suite. I am also familiar with regular web Browsers, Photoshop and AutoCAD."

**OR**

- "Among the Operating Systems, I am proficient in Windows NT, Windows XP, Windows ME, Mac 0SX, Windows 2000, Mac OS 8.6, Solaris, Mac 0S9, UNIX, Linux, AIX, Sun OS, OS/2, DOS, FreeBSD, Novell 4.0, Exchange 5.5, etc. Among software solutions,
- I am proficient in Microsoft Office Suite, IE, Outlook Express, Lotus 1-2-3, IBM Notes, etc. I also have good knowledge of Adobe Photoshop, Corel Draw Pro, Adobe

Illustrator, Studio, FileMaker Pro, MySQL, SQL Server, SQL 6.5 & 7.0, Enterprise Manager, EZ-SQL, Net Objects Fusion, Vignette, Broad Vision, etc.

## 45. On a scale of 1 to 10, how would you rate yourself as a leader?

Interview questions and answers are a way of testing you in and out. The interviewer may ask you this question to gauge your self-confidence.

### Sample Answers

- "I rate my leadership skills an 8 out of 10. There is much to learn, but I have always been a strong leader. I was the head boy/girl during my school days, and in college, I was a Senior Wing NCC Cadet. I have completed my C-certificate and have earned lots of badges in several NCC camps. I have led the Senior Boys/Girls contingent at the Republic Day Camp in 2012 as well."

**OR**

- "I am a good leader. That is the reason why today, I manage a 5-member strong team independently in an MNC. While assigning tasks, I consider people skills often. If a team member is feeling demotivated, I try my level best to understand them and accordingly control the situation. Bearing my performance as a manager over the past few years, I would rate myself an 8.5/10, as there is still a lot of scope to learn and grow."

## 46. Are you open to take risks? or Do you like experimenting?

**Sample Answer**

- "It is always good to venture into new waters and new technologies. I am a very adaptive person, and my diligence helps me pick up new stuff quickly. Experimenting or taking risks can yield both good and bad results, but the exercise in itself is a great learning experience. Such experiences generate experts, and I want to become an SME or a JAVA subject matter expert someday."

**OR**

- "This is a good question and a complex one. My answer would be both a No and a Yes. Personally, I like to experiment with new things, but I keep all my past mistakes in mind before taking a shot at a brand-new project. For example, carpentry is my hobby and I love to build small furniture pieces with my new toolkit, which was a gift from my brother. But I will never venture into a complete home renovation project with that little kit! What I mean to say is that baby steps are fine, but I will not jump off a cliff at once."

## 47. What are your future goals? Tell me about your short term and long-term goals.

**Sample Answer**

- "My short-term goal is to join a reputed company, like yours, where my job role would allow me to apply my knowledge and key strengths. I want to get recognized for my contribution to the company in the long-run."

OR

- "I've picked up the Marketing Automation basics during my first job, which lasted for two years. Now I am prepared to take up a bigger and more challenging project. I want to see myself as a marketing analyst in the next two years, that would be my short-term goal. Following this, I would see myself as an end-to-end Digital Marketing Strategist or a Manager in the long run."

## 48. Why do you want to change job?

The hiring manager is looking to understand more about your job performance and history, as well as learn more about your own motivations. All of this information helps the employer get a better sense of whether you'll be a good fit for the company and also helps the company determine whether you have any red flags that it should be aware of. This question will likely come up if you're still employed so be prepared with a great answer in order to get the job.

*Points to Emphasize*

- Remain positive about your current job and employer. Highlight the things you like about the job before emphasizing why you're seeking better opportunities elsewhere.
- Provide specific details about what motivates you to apply for this particular position and how you can use your previous experience to benefit your potential employer.
- As your response winds down, end on a strong note by reiterating how you will bring valued skills and experience to the new position.
- Always remain collegial and polite and never get defensive. Even if you can't wait to leave your current job, keep these thoughts to yourself.
- Having a ready and thoughtful answer to this question can help elevate you to the head of the pack in the hiring manager's mind.

*Mistakes You Should Avoid*

This question can be difficult to answer if you are experiencing speed bumps in your current job. Below are a few pointers to help you craft a great response even when your job is less than perfect.

- Never show desperation to leave your job or display overt negativity about your previous employer. Emphasize at least one positive quality about your current job and focus on the skills you gained, rather than the problems you faced.
- Don't forget to discuss your overall career goals and how the new job will fit into that plan.
- When comparing your current job with the one you are seeking, provide details and concrete anecdotes to show your logic in wanting to make a transition.
- Be sure you have a ready response to this question; otherwise, you may risk sounding evasive.

## 49. What do you know about our company?

The interviewer wants to know if you:

- have done your research about their company;
- can describe the company well as an informed outsider; and
- can translate what you know about the company into expressing interest. The question is, in effect, a reverse sell. It may be the setup question for the interviewer selling you on the company, with the question acting as

- the baseline for what additional information they may need to tell you about.
- Know the employer well enough to be able to succinctly describe it in 30-60 seconds. Don't just take it for granted that you know the employer, do actual in-depth research., turn the question into a why are you interested response.

*Sample answer*: "I'm an Amazon customer and have been for many years. But I know that Amazon is much more than the consumer retail side and the focus on price, selection, and convenience. The company also includes Amazon Web Services for Cloud Computing, products such as Kindle, Fire, and Echo, and many of the Prime-related activities in entertainment. There are many different parts of Amazon that I find to be fascinating and would love the opportunity to be part of the organization..."

## 50. What do you like about our company?

When you go into a room for a professional interview, the interviewer wants to learn more about you, but he or she also wants to see how much you already know about the enterprise. For instance, the hiring manager may ask, "What do you like most about this company" The point of this question is to ascertain your overall career goals and whether or not the position is an integral part of your professional plan. In short, are you truly motivated to acquire this position and will you give your best work after being hired to Treat this as an opportunity to show genuine enthusiasm for not just the position but also for working in the company? Think about when you applied for this position. What was the deciding factor in that choice Use this in your response?

- Focus on your professional goals and align them with the company.
- Mention anything specific such as company leaders, market position or values.
- Emphasize the company's positive work and/or outreach.
- Concentrate on the real reasons why you applied.

The number one rule is staying positive. Show your enthusiasm and your knowledge of the company.

**Sample answer:** "Well, first and foremost, I would say the company's overall reputation drew me in. I've been in finance for ten years and XYZ Company has always been an industry leader in innovation and community-friendly standards. I've had a few friends and family members who either worked here or with the business and they've always raved about the atmosphere of professionalism. I look forward to being in a place that continually demands excellence while still allowing a healthy and positive work environment."

Remember, focus on why you want the job and the real reasons this company is on your list of prospective employers. Lastly, let your enthusiasm shine through in your answer.

## 51. Where do you see yourself in 5 years?

This is one question that employers use to trap you in a corner and you may not even recognize it at all. Employers don't just ask this question because they are really interested in what you want to do with your life in 5 years' time, they simply want to know your career goals within the position.

The hiring manager is interested in knowing how satisfied you are with the position and the company and how hard and long you are willing to grow and stay in the company. Employers ask this question for two reasons:

- The employer wants to know how long you plan to stay in the position.
- The employer wants to know if your vision aligns with that of the company.

**Sample answer:** "In 5 years, I would love to complete my internal and external training program for my position. I have read about it on your website, and I think it is an amazing opportunity for me to learn. I don't only look forward to getting the right training for my role, but it will quicken my journey to becoming a marketing manager which my career goal. My ideal track would be creating awareness in rural areas. I learned that getting your product to rural places is of great value to you."

## 52. What's your salary expectation?

Interviewers ask about your salary requirements for different reasons. Some interviewers will ask about your salary requirement because they want to know if it matches what they are ready to afford. It is always important for you to be careful about your response to this question so that you don't get underpaid at the end of the day. When you are answering this question, take note of the following:

Make sure you have researched the salary range for your position before going for the interview

Always give a range and avoid giving a clear cut answer

Be flexible

You should also avoid Blurting out a salary range

**Sample answer**: "I think I am looking at something in the range of N100-N150, I believe that is the range this company offers for my level of employment. I think I am comfortable with the range".

## 53. If we were to celebrate our first year in the company, what would be the greatest result we could celebrate?

Accomplishments are the stars of the show when it comes to job interviews. Most interview questions can be answered with an accomplishments story, and employers will appreciate it if you tell these stories copiously because they provide solid examples of the qualifications hiring managers seek -- whether skills, experience, values, subject-matter expertise, industry knowledge, or other criteria

**Sample answer:** "Anyone can say they do a better job than others, and at this level, I certainly hope there is at least some truth in that belief. But rather than simply saying, yes, I can transform the marketing functions of this company better than anyone else can, let me give you an example of why I am confident I can do a better job than any other candidate. As the marketing director for Hansen Beverage Company, I built on the founding family's early but regional successes with high-quality all-natural beverages and leveraged the marketplace by introducing new products and expanding distribution nationally".

## 54. Have you done other job interviews?

This question always throws people for a loop. Why are they asking, and how much do they actually need to know? Well, hiring managers are curious about what other companies you're interviewing with for a few reasons. They might want to scope out the competition, see how serious you are about the industry, or even gauge their likelihood of landing such a star candidate. So, how do you respond to this in a way that doesn't make you sound desperate or unattainable? Here are some ideas, depending on your particular situation. You know not to say this directly, but how do you get around it? The trick is to simply choose to answer a different question. Instead of responding with your lack of other interviews, let your interviewer know what types of positions and companies you've been applying to.

**Sample Answer**: I'm still pretty early in my job search. I've applied to a number of opportunities that will allow me to use my skills in data visualization to help educate clients, but this position is most exciting to me. In fact, I think this position is a particularly good fit for my skill set because I can leverage my significant experience working with complicated data sets."

## 55. What are your professional aspirations?

A hiring manager will ask this to determine if you are likely to stay with the company in the future. For example, if you want to advance to a position that is taken by a tenured individual, the interviewer now knows that your time with the enterprise is limited. This is not necessary and the most important question in the interview. After all, it maybe five years before you qualify for a management position, which gives you plenty of time to provide the company with quality work. Show the interviewer that you have put some thought into your professional career. He or she will be impressed if you can concisely and clearly answer the question.

Briefly touch on short-term goals if you haven't had the chance to address them.

- Focus on your overall trajectory assuming you are a successful employee.
- Highlight your ambition to develop professionally.
- Remain reasonable in your aspirations.

Here, you need to strike a balance between ambition and realism. Focus on the attributes of your future position such as project oversight, working closely with important clients or creative problem-solving. Remember to incorporate the position into your long-term goals. Even if it is just a stepping-stone, make an effort to show a genuine interest in the company and the job.

**Sample answer:** 'In the short term, I'd like to become an expert in my position and learn more about this sector of the industry. In the long term, I want to focus on understanding the industry as a whole so that I can advance to a management level position. My ultimate goal is to work closely with the company's clientele and oversee major projects'

## 56. Are you willing to relocate?

First impressions are crucial in an interview, but so is how you answer their questions. Each answer to every question that is relentlessly hurled at you impacts the final decision. Are you confident in your response? Is your answer honest? Do you struggle in your responses? Interviewers are looking for these signs along with your answer. But what about the question that often asked and could have an effect on the hiring process, are you willing to relocate? This question could come as a surprise or you could have been prepared for it. But what should your response be? Here are five responses that will make sure your name is not removed from consideration;

"I am absolutely willing to relocate". This might be the obvious answer, especially if you are able to relocate anywhere they would like. As a young adult, the opportunity to relocate might be exciting. Answering that you are definitely willing to relocate will show that you want to do whatever is necessary to be a part of the company and team.

A formal answer would be: "For the right opportunity I am definitely willing to relocate. I believe that this position and company is that opportunity."

Relocating for a job is a major life change. There are many questions left unanswered that could cause you to debate whether you are willing to move for a position. How long will you be there?

Is this a company I want to have a long career with? Will I be able to advance my career with positions? All of these questions would have anyone on the fence about relocating for a job. So can you answer maybe? The answer is yes, maybe is an answer and not a bad one. It is how you answer that is important. You might respond with:

"I very much enjoy this area and would love to continue my career here, but this position is a great opportunity for my career and if relocating is a part of that, I would definitely consider it."

"Moving is not always that ideal situation. Though this job opportunity might be exactly what you are looking for, moving still does not get you excited. Most companies will ask if you are willing to relocate to gauge your interest in the position. This question could be a major factor in determining if you are hired. This is where honesty is important. Lying in an interview is bad for all parties involved"

It is ok to be hesitant about relocating. It is important to portray that in the best way possible in the interview. Answering with a statement like, "This is a great opportunity and a position I believe I am a great fit. I enjoy working in this area, but I would consider relocating depending on the circumstances."

This will help you stay on track while staying honest with the interviewer. They will see that you are willing to do what it takes to be a part of the team and would like to further your career at this location.

Sometimes moving is just not an option. Several reasons could cause a need for you to stay in this area. But if you say no will it cause you to lose this job opportunity? In some cases, it just might. But there is a way to say no without insinuating you don't want the job.

"This is a great opportunity for my career and would love to be a part of the team here. I enjoy this area and think it is where I would like to further my career, especially with this company." This could be a great answer that states that moving is not something that you would like to do, but you are sincere about wanting the job. Being honest can get you far with a potential employer.

With very few correct answers to this job, there are a plethora of wrong answers. You will not know every answer in an interview. In fact, they don't necessarily expect you to know every answer throughout the interview. Even when you don't know the answer, there still is a correct response. When asked if you are willing to relocate there are many wrong answers. Let's take a look at what not to say:

"Are you going to pay me more?"

"If I get to choose where you move me."

"I never want to move from this area."

"Depends on what you are willing to offer."

Any answers along these lines will make them forget about you and move on to the next candidate. Some of the best advice that I have ever heard states, "It is not necessarily what you say but how you say it that is more important." This is definitely true during an interview when you are answering certain questions.

## 57. What do you think your tasks will be?

In an interview, your potential employer's ultimate goal is to assess if the position is a good fit for you. One way your interviewer might go about this is to figure out which aspects of the job will be the toughest for you to master. The best way to approach this question is to analyze the job at hand and think about which tasks will be most difficult for you based on your past experiences.

Start by breaking down the job into its various components and thinking about the skills, knowledge, and experiences you would need to master each component. You should also think about elements of the job that will require learning or adjustments you'll need to make. Make sure to match your qualifications to the position's requirements. If possible, you should also discuss how you might get yourself up to speed in the least amount of time. For example, you might take a course, complete online training, or take seminars on a topic you need help with.

## 58. How did you find this job?

You may have found the opportunity through research on ideal jobs where you can make the most impact and hope to grow professionally. I would also hope you looked for companies that you feel meet your standards for corporate culture, investment in employees, successful business model (or perhaps giving back to the community), and any other aspects you feel are important to you.

Make sure you can go into a little detail on what you found in your research. The "job" may have found you. In that case, you can say HR contacted you or a recruiter who felt you were a good fit. But don't leave it there. You should still mention you did your homework and verified that this is right for you as a potential contributor to the company's success, and as a good match for what you're looking for in an employer.

## 59. Are You Willing To Travel For The Job?

"Are you willing to travel?" is a common question, one you may encounter on your next job interview. If a hiring manager asks you if you are willing to travel for the job, it may set off alarm bells. You could worry that you'll be overburdened with extensive travel responsibilities that take you away from home. What makes this question even more challenging is that it tends to come very early in the job interview process. In most cases, the job description contains information about travel, so hopefully, this question will not catch you by complete surprise. You'll likely know a little bit about the travel requirement before applying and should set aside some time to think through this question in advance of your first interview.

When the hiring manager asks this question, they are looking to gauge your willingness to travel—and the extent to which you will travel for the job. Often, the hiring manager will explain the travel requirements for the job during your interview, after you answer the question regarding willingness. The hiring manager will share their expectations with you so that you can decide whether or not the position is a good fit for you.

Hiring managers primarily want to know that you are open to travel experiences outside of the office when asking the question "Are you willing to travel?" You can help the manager know that you understand the necessity of travel in the normal function of the company by answering the question openly and honestly. At the point when you answer the question "Are you ready to travel?" you need to underscore your positive encounters with travel. What's more, you have to keep up a positive tone when doing as such.

- Share data about how travel in past occupations has profited your instruction or expert preparing
- Accentuate your promise to finishing your activity duties, paying little mind to where the activity may take you

- Notice that travel builds an organization's organizing limit
- Clarify how travel grows your expert chances

Aim to provide a general answer, one that does not make the hiring manager feel as though travel burdens your life. You also do not want to define an amount of travel, for that will affect the hiring manager's ability to consider you for the job. If your number is even slightly below the company's expectation, it can label you as not interested in the job. If you are not prepared for the "Are you willing to travel?" question, you might easily focus on the negatives and make some of the following mistakes.

- Do not complain about travel or talk about past misfortunes in airports, or at hotels
- Be careful not to explain that you enjoy sight-seeing or going on vacation while on business travel
- Do not ask questions about or discuss the option to bring your spouse or children with you on business travel
- Avoid going into descriptions of your family or personal responsibilities
- Do not give a specific maximum percentage of preferred travel
- Do not ask questions about travel reimbursement or travel policies these questions can be asked (and will be answered) at a later time

**Sample Answers**

"Yes, I'm willing to travel. Travel in my previous jobs has allowed me to go to special conferences and Strainings that have expanded my knowledge of our industry. I always strive to be an asset to the company for which I work—if travel is needed to help the company succeed, I'm definitely game for traveling."

**OR**

"I'm definitely willing to travel. I've been looking for a job that will allow me to travel as part of my responsibilities because I find that travel allows me to expand my knowledge of the many facets of a company's customer base. Travel allows me to not only grow my education, but also my professional network."

## 60. Discuss your resume

Briefly explain the key contents of your resume such as the relevant jobs you have held, your key tasks and major accomplishments.

Specifically, focus on the experience that directly relates to the job you are interviewing for. Also, talk about your educational qualifications and your top skills and areas of specialization.

**Example**: "My most current role that relates to the Information Systems Manager position was working as a Technical Assistant at company XYZ where I was involved in training users, repairing computer hardware and installing software. I held a 95% percent customer satisfaction rating for two years for promptly responding and supporting 60 users. Prior to that, I had worked as an intern for three months at a local manufacturing plant where I supported two Information Technology Managers in troubleshooting and fixing office equipment.

I have a Degree in Information Technology and my key areas of expertise are network security and computer troubleshooting."

## 61. Explain a gap in your employment?

Sometimes a gap in your employment or career is inevitable. If there is a gap in your employment, you might be asked for an explanation. A gap in employment can arise due to many factors such as being laid off, getting fired, inability to find a suitable job, going back to school, resignation, and relocation.

Other factors for a gap are taking a sabbatical, volunteering, career change, sickness/medical reasons, taking care of a loved one or taking time to start a family or raise children.

Any of the above items is a valid reason. Briefly and honestly mention the reason for the gap and highlight that you are looking forward to re-join the workforce with great energy to make a positive contribution to your new role.

**Example**: "I was out of work for 6 months last year to pursue an intensive Creative Design certification course. I realized that I needed to invest in this training and knowledge to stay up to date with state of the art technology changes in the design field and to position myself for future high level and high impact positions in my field. I look forward to test-driving my new skills in this position."

## 62. If you were to create a company what will be the 3 core values

Even if you don't directly get asked this question, the interviewer is interviewing you to find out what value you can add to the company. Be prepared to answer, tailor your answer to your "fit" with the company. Honestly, look at your strengths and the job requirements, and highlight where they align. Give examples.

For example, if you:

- Have been in the industry a long time, highlight your experience, and give a few examples of how you can bring your expertise to add value.
- Know people who work at the company, highlight your cultural fit. Give examples of the traits you share in common, and how important it is for you to add to the culture.

- Use the product, highlight your passion for its use. Give examples of how your knowledge of the product will help you to add value.
- I already work at the company and are looking to move positions. Give examples of all the processes you understand and how your knowledge coming from the x department will help augment the value in the z department.

## 63. If you were to create a company what will be the motto

When asking this question, interviewers are trying to get back to the essence of what the question was originally used for. They want to see if you are truly committed to a career. If you can demonstrate a clear career desire that aligns with the company's goals, you can stand out amongst other applicants.

In answering this question there are a few things that you should be aware of and do.

- If you have a mission statement on your resume, try to recant it as closely as possible.
- Tailor your response to the position that you are applying for.
- Show a desire to grow and establish a career.
- Make sure that you can provide support or proof for all parts of your statement.

- Try not to make your answer lengthy, but be sure to paint a clear picture of your mission, and make sure that it coincides with the position you are applying for.

Answering this question incorrectly can reflect negatively on you and hinder your chances of securing the job. Try to avoid the following mistakes.

- Do not give a general, predictable answer that could be applied to any position.
- Stay away from making your mission statement about the company.
- Do not give a short, vague response.
- Even if you are strong in certain skills, do not focus your mission statement on them if they do not relate to the position at hand.

## 64. Tell me about a time at work when your integrity was challenged. How did you handle it?

Have you ever faced a time, in the workplace, where you were put to the test when it came to your integrity? Perhaps a co-worker has asked you to lie, or you were tempted to be dishonest on your timesheet when the boss was away. Talk to the interviewer about a time when you overcame the temptation to be dishonest.

### Sample Answer

"My manager once asked us to lead our teams in a direction that was not in alignment with the overall department's mission and values. As a results-oriented person, I typically switch into high gear to accomplish the work. When I gave it thought, I realized it was against our best interests and brought my concerns to the leadership team. Together, we formulated a plan to meet the objective and still behave by our vision and values."

"I once had a customer accuse me of lying about our return policy. We had just changed it but had not update the website yet. I felt sad that someone would accuse me of lying. The situation was repaired quickly, thank goodness."

# HYPOTHETICAL QUESTIONS

Much the same as conduct interview questions, HR chiefs pose these inquiries to discover how the applicant will act in a specific circumstance. Interviewers pose these inquiries so they can have a thought of the applicant's point of view on how he/she will deal with a specific circumstance when looked with one. A theoretical interview question similarly as the name infers is a circumstance whereby the selection representatives place the up-and-comer in a non-existent circumstance to perceive how they would deal with the circumstance. Interviewers pose this inquiry to investigate the up-and-comer's explanatory abilities. Read this before answering hypothetic interview questions:

- Don't be in a hurry to answer
- Stay calm and put yourself together before answering the question
- You can give examples to make the interviewer understand your thought process
- Take your time, and respond to the interviewer confidently

## 65. How would you handle it if the priorities for a project you were working on were suddenly changed?

When interviews ask this question, they want to know how you would act in that particular situation. The interviewer wants to know how you would act if that particular situation shows up. The interviewer will also want to know your problem-solving skills. You should prove to the interviewer that you can successfully figure out a solution to a problem. Always make the interviewer understand your thought process.

When you are answering this question, you should take note of the following:

Show the interviewer how well you can handle the pressure

Show the interviewer the skills and abilities you possess that will help you perform the job better.

**Sample Answer:** "Well, I understand that at some points the vision that one may want to achieve doing a project may change due to different reasons. So if the priority of a project that I am working on changes, I would not get myself worked up over the change, I will rather understand that it is for the best interest of the company and that we must continue to put in our best to achieve great results. The first practical thing I will do is to make sure that I understand why the priorities were changed, how I would adjust to this change putting in my best effort".

Answering this question this way shows the interviewer that you have a positive attitude, and that you can work well under pressure.

## 66. What would you do if you disagreed with the way a manager wanted you to handle a problem?

When interviewers ask this question, they want to know how you deal with a superior and how you express your disagreement on a particular issue.

The hiring manager knows that disagreement happens, so they are not trying to make you feel bad for being in that situation, they simply want to know if you have a good relationship with people in authority.

Your relationship with your manager or supervisor says a lot about you as a person.

- When you are answering this question, you should focus on skills and experience that helped you dissolve the disagreement.

**Sample Answer:** "If I disagree with the way my manager wants me to handle a project I will walk up to my manager and explain why I think that is not the best approach, then I will give him/her good reasons why I think that my approach is the best for this project.

I believe that communication is key, and communicating my ideas respectfully with my manager is what will help us have a single vision on a project. If I see the reasons why my manager's idea is the best for the project, then I would admit that too. I believe communication is the key".

## 67. Who are your references?

You are expected to have references who can provide independent assessments and recommendations about your skills, abilities, qualifications, work performance, working style, professional character, etc.

Typically, professional references would include supervisors, subordinates, work colleagues, professors, teachers, business partners, customers or clients. Choose references that know you and can give the best possible feedback.

They should be able to talk about specifics rather than giving general feedback about you and your work abilities. It is a good practice to give an updated copy of your resume to your references.

In addition, it is strategic to give your references a heads-up when you are interviewing for jobs so that they can be alert when contacted for a reference.

**Example**: "My three references are two of my former bosses, one at Company A where I worked as a Senior Editor and the other at Company B where I worked as an Editor and also one colleague who I worked closely with at Company C."

## 68. What would your references say about you?

Your response to this question will be determined by the type of references you have.

You could have different categories of references such as supervisors, subordinates, co-workers, business partners, customers, clients, suppliers, vendors, and academic references. Each category sees you and interacts with you in a different capacity. Below are a few pointers on what supervisors, subordinates, co-workers, customers, suppliers, and academic references would say about you.

A supervisor can comment on how you work, how you follow direction, your punctuality, creativity, teamwork, problem-solving ability, positive attitude, taking initiative, productivity, flexibility, meeting deadlines, etc.

Subordinates would speak about what type of boss you were. They can talk about your leadership style, how you motivate staff and provide feedback, your communication style, vision, accessibility, offering praise and recognition, etc.

Work colleagues would remark about what kind of a co-worker you were. Your willingness to help, your knowledge and expertise, empathy, collaboration, team player, hard worker, dependability, integrity, work ethic, etc.

Customers or clients could talk about your customer service skills, listening skills, presentation skills, following up, meeting deadlines, quality of work or service provided, enthusiasm, etc.

Suppliers or vendors could discuss your planning skills, attention to detail, fairness, integrity, communication, work standards, etc.

Whereas academic references can offer feedback on how hardworking you were in class, your curiosity to learn, participation, teamwork, communication, and presentation skills, taking feedback and correction, self-drive and desire to succeed, etc. Your reference list should include at least three references. It should list your name and contact details at the top of the document.

List the names, current titles, organization and contact details such as email and telephone.

Next, add a brief description below each reference identifying the nature of your relationship such as "was my former boss at company XYZ."The description is beneficial especially since people change jobs and companies over time.

**Example**: "My supervisory references would say that I was known for completing multiple production projects and schedules against tight deadlines. They will describe that as a Production Assistant at Company XYZ, I supported a busy production team in filming and editing documentaries and live events. I was also commended by my supervisor for piloting a podcast that quickly took off and became a regularly scheduled program. My supervisors and co-workers would also describe me as an easy-going person who gets along easily with colleagues and clients."

## 69. How would you handle working closely with a colleague who was very different from you?

The interviewer understands the idea of workplace diversity, so the interviewer may ask you this question to find out how well you can accommodate other people that are quite different from you. The interviewer may ask you this question to find out if you can work in a team.

Employers look forward to getting candidates that can function well in a team

**Sample Answer:** "I understand that there is diversity in the workplace, and I am open to embracing and accepting people the way they are. In my previous position, I was working closely with a colleague that is really reserved and accommodates little communication, and I love to ask questions and communicate a lot. At first, I did not find it interesting talking with my colleague, but later I discovered that she loves to work with little or no distraction at all and I understood and accepted her that way. Her reserved nature helped me complete my task even faster. Since then I learned to value and accept differences".

## 70. How would you handle an instance of receiving criticism from a superior?

Interviewers always ask this question most times because they want to know how you handle the pressure that comes from work. Interviewers understand what it is like to face criticism especially when it is coming to a supervisor, so the interviewer wants to know how you can handle criticism.

As a job-seeker, you should know that the interviewer wants to know how you handle criticism if you take it in the positive or negative light.

You should avoid:

- You should avoid being overwhelmed by the criticism
- Avoid giving the impression that you hate to be criticized

**Sample Answer**: "I welcome constructive criticism because I feel it is a way to make me do better. In my previous job, my boss always criticized me that I don't communicate well, I did not feel down by his comment I rather got to know that It was a problem I had to fix, and I am happy he brought that problem to my notice, it has really helped. I appreciate constructive criticism a lot".

## 71. Tell me about a time you reached a big goal at work. How did you reach it?

Employers love employees that look forward to achieving something in the future and not people that merely want to complete tasks and get paid for that. Interviewers are interested in getting hires that can set goals and achieve them eventually.

When interviewers ask this question, they are interested in knowing if you are the kind of person that sets achievable goals and dedicate your time to actually achieve those goals. The interviewer is also interested in how you were able to achieve the goals you set.

When you are answering this question, you should give an instance of career-related goals.

Always remember to take note of the following when you are answering this question:

- Choose your most remarkable achieved goal
- Tell the interviewer how you achieved the goal
- Talk about what you have learned from the experience
- Let the interviewer be aware of how you are going to apply the lessons that you have learned

You should also avoid:

- Avoid talking about goals that are not career-related

- Avoid giving answers like "I have never set a big goal to talk of achieving success"

**Sample Answer:** "This year I set a goal for myself to successfully increase the company sales from 40% to 60% and to also increase our customer retention rate. I dedicated myself to researching and taking courses on different marketing strategies that would likely work. I also had to work extra hours aside from work hours. At the end of the year, the company sales moved from 40% to 72% and our customer retention rate also increased too".

## 72. What would you do if you worked hard on a solution to a problem, and your solution was criticized by your team?

Interviewers understand that situations that may lead to disagreement may likely come up, so they are expecting that those kinds of information will not come up. What interviewers are interested in is how you would handle such a situation when they arise.

With your answers to this question, the interviewer wants to know how you handle criticism and your approach to dealing with different people. When you are answering this question, you should take note of the following:

- Let the interviewer know how you handle criticism

- Tell the interviewer know how you handle the criticism that you got
- Talk about what you learned from the criticism with the interviewer

You should also avoid:

- Avoid showing off any form of anger and resentment
- Avoid giving a response like "I am a perfectionist and I am very careful about my work, so I don't think anyone in the right state of mind will criticize anything that I do".

**Sample Answer:** "I totally understand that we all look, but see things differently. So if I am approaching a solution from a different perspective that I think is the best, one that I assume will provide the best solution and my team members disagreed with it despite the hard work that I have put into it.

The best thing I can do is to understand what the criticism is all about, see from their own point of view and take note of things I did not do right. In my previous place of work, we noticed that our sales for the month dropped, so we were thinking of how to come up with a solution to grow our sales, I came up with strategies and advert campaigns, my team members criticized it and at the end I got to understand that we did not have enough financial resources to run paid adverts etc.

From that project, I learned to communicate my ideas with my team members before I take a decision to avoid time wastage".

## NON-CONVENTIONAL QUESTIONS

### 73. If you were an animal, what would it be?

Many interviewers ask this (odd) interview questions for different reasons, and not because they just want to joke with you. Interviewers ask this question because they want to have an idea about your personality type, asking you this question, they are simply asking you to describe yourself using an animal. Some interviewers ask this question because they want to understand your thought process and your level of creativity. When you are answering this question, take note of the following:

- Always consider the job role before you choose an animal
- Make sure the characteristics of the animal that you have chosen match your skills and abilities
- Be careful that the characteristics of the animal matches the job description

You should also avoid choosing animals with known poor qualities and opposing characteristics to the job role

**Example:** "If I were to be an animal, I would be a lion. A lion always loves challenges and does not like to be spoon fed. A lion knows what it wants and goes for it. I thrive with challenges, and I think that a lion better describes me".

*Animals and their traits*

- Elephant: Elephant trunks are capable of doing many hard-core jobs that are not limited to breathing or water spraying.
- Dolphin: Dolphins are known for their self-sacrifice and selflessness. They are the best rescue team of all time. Even during times when they find someone is injured or needs help, they always initiate.
- Cows: One can easily compare the similarities by counting oneself as the cow and show their loyalty towards the company they will work for in the future.
- Dogs: Dogs are known for their loyal features and friendly nature all around the world.
- Lions: Yes, the king of the jungle stands tall and ready to fight. Moreover, even after being strong and mighty they never leave the hand of their pack.
- Butterfly: Always in one stage or another of development, waiting for your day to fly.
- Owl: Very wise, very good at seeing the big picture, very good at getting what it wants
- Ant: Hard worker
- Chameleon: Blends in well, not one to stand out, very sneaky

- Dove: A peacemaker, always looking for the non-violent solution

## 74. How would you fire an employee?

It's unlikely that the interviewer is thirsty for corporate blood, and looking for a kindred spirit. Rather, firing people is an unfortunate fact of life at any company. If you're interviewing for any kind of management position or a position that has the potential to grow into the management level, it's a valid test of your future management skills.

If you recoil and say, "Oh, I could never fire anyone," you could look like a pushover. If you go the opposite way and talk about how much you love firing people, you could come off more like a sociopath than a tough boss. This isn't a test to see how badass you can be. It's a test to see how you would handle a real-life situation. You don't get extra points for making the metaphorical fired person cry, so make sure you keep a neutral, professional tone. Very few companies are looking for a tyrant to fill a position.

Firing individuals is a sensitive area, yet it is also mandatory at times. You have to be able to strike a balance. In that vein, be sure to evade these mistakes.

- Avoid sounding as if you are excited about the idea of firing someone.
- Do not sound timid or unwilling to fulfill the duty.

- Do not question the circumstances revolving the situation; give a clear answer.
- Steer clear of giving a cut and dry answer (that can make you seem uncaring).

Though it may be tricky, it is important to find the middle ground between non-caring and excessively eager.

**Example:** First, I would consult with HR about the appropriate protocol. Second, I would then inform the employee of their termination, stating the things that they did well along with those that they did poorly. Finally, I would allow them to ask any questions to ensure that any confusion or issues are addressed.

## 75. If you could start a business, what would you do?

A revealing interview question is asked in order to ascertain some revealing information about the job candidate that he or she wouldn't normally offer during the conversation. A hiring manager asks a basic question that seems simple, yet the candidate's answer will reveal vital information. This type of question can be perceived as one that is meant to trick the candidate. However, a practical hiring manager knows that it is sometimes necessary to ask revealing questions in order to figure out who is the best candidate for the job. Basically, the hiring manager needs to ascertain if the candidate makes any contradictory statements during the interview.

These questions are used to wade through the "fluff" and discover the genuine self of the candidate. In addition to discovering the genuine center of the candidate, the hiring manager is also trying to ascertain the individual's reaction to being asked such a question. For example, if the individual becomes defensive or evasive, that can become a warning sign to the hiring manager that this person may not be the best candidate for the job. A third factor in being asked this question is that the hiring manager wants to ascertain your reliability and consistency. For example, you could possibly grow bored with the work and quit the job if you have aspirations to start your own business.

When crafting a response to this question remember to keep three factors in mind. You need to be authentic, non-aggressive, and to demonstrate your reliability. Remove the complexity of the question by crafting an answer that responds to the basic factor of entrepreneurship and whether or not it is part of your life. Consider the following sample responses:

- If you have an entrepreneurial penchant, you need to demonstrate this in a positive light to the hiring manager. For example, don't say that you want to start a business in the next few years. You can share that you have worked as an independent contractor in the past or have cultivated some entrepreneurial ventures. However, ensure that you make this a positive trait that can positively influence your future with the company.

- If you have never considered starting your own business, you can be completely honest about that fact and demonstrate that there are no downsides to that factor in your life. With regard to this answer, you have the chance to share that you value working as an employee in a corporate or small business workplace setting. In crafting your answer, you can alleviate any fears that the hiring manager may have by demonstrating your partiality for being part of a team environment without having to concern yourself with running a business.

## 76. If someone wrote a biography about you, what would the title be?

Everybody likes a creative, team player, and this question can tell an employer more about those two things than you might think. The titles of autobiographies range from mundane to intriguing, and some are more arrogant than others. For example, if you say the title should be "How I Made My Millions," it will make you look a lot more arrogant and unoriginal than if you choose the more humble and creative "Are We There Yet?" which shows humility and creativity most employers want in their interviewees.

Essentially, the key to mastering the strangest of interview questions is getting to the heart of each question and understanding exactly what the interviewer wants you to say. Each answer should aim to show your strengths, even when it seems ridiculous.

## 77. If you were a survivor on a deserted island, what one person would you like to have with you?

This question is one of the oldest in the book, and it's asked during "get-to-know-you activities" and "trust-building exercises" about as often as in job interviews. It's generally asked in an attempt to gauge your problem-solving skills. For example, if you say you'd like to have Justin Bieber with you, you're in for some great entertainment, but will probably be on the island for a while.

However, if you were to say, Benjamin Franklin, that would send a different message to your employers. It lets them know that you recognize the value of an independent thinker who isn't afraid to work his inventive magic to get the job done, despite ridicule. When you're asked this question at a job interview, be thinking of a true problem-solver you admire and the reasons you admire them.

## 78. Which superhero could defeat any other superhero?

The value of this question is that it allows the employer an opportunity to assess your personality, which can be an important factor in any work environment. The answer largely depends on where you're working. If you're looking for an upbeat, relaxed environment, it's okay to get a little competitive and say, "Batman, he has the coolest toys so he will win every time."

If you're working in a more serious, uptight environment, it's still okay to show your fun side. However, keep the answer more rooted in logic such as, "According to science, the Hulk would have to win because he is virtually indestructible."

If you're not sure, go for a diplomatic approach such as, "I like to think that true superhero would never go into battle against their own. In the end, they would all end up fighting for the same cause."

Furthermore, remember that it's often appropriate to ask questions of clarification before answering a question like this one. Questions might include:

- "Where is the fight taking place?"
- "Is kryptonite fair game?"
- "Do they have special weapons?"

This shows that you are actively considering the question and working through all your options to determine the most probable outcome. It ultimately shows that you have a problem-solving aptitude.

## 79. Sell me this pen

This is a typical role-playing exercise that is conducted in interviews so that the hiring manager can learn about your sales technique and thought process. You may be asked to sell the interviewer a stapler, piece of paper or anything else, but the basic process should be the same. This is not the chance for you to talk about the skills you would use in a hypothetical situation. Use this opportunity to assume your salesman persona and actually try to sell the person sitting across from you this pencil.

- Regardless of what you are trying to sell, you need to keep the following points in mind.
- Focus on what the customer needs rather than aspects of the item
- Ask questions to gain insight into what the customer needs
- Relate what the pencil can do to what the customer needs
- Always close the deal at the end

This can be a make-or-break moment in a lot of interviews. Nailing it can instantly getting you the job while underperforming seriously jeopardizes your chances. Being asked to sell something during an interview is extremely common if you are applying for a sales position, so prepare beforehand so that you are ready if this comes up.

**Sample Answer**

An exchange for this sales pitch should go something like this:

Let me ask you something: how often do you use a pencil

(Pretty frequently)

And are you happy with the pencils you are currently using

(They're fine)

I don't think something you use as frequently as you say should be just "fine." I think you should have a pencil that offers exceptional results. A pencil that doesn't break and ruins the aesthetic of whatever it is that you are writing. This pencil gets the job done right every time.

(Sounds pretty good)

All I'm asking is that you give this pencil a shot. If you aren't completely satisfied, feel free to bring it back, and I'll give you a full refund.

The exchange does not have to go exactly like this, but it should follow the basic points listed above.

## 80. Tell Me a Story.

Find out what kind of story the interviewer wants to hear. Asking for clarification shows you are thoughtful and won't go on wild goose chases in the office if difficult projects aren't spelled out for you in advance. Once you learn the type of story requested, create your very short tale around a time that you accomplished something great. Keep it short and sweet, and remember: Always make yourself look good. Think of this as the interviewer, "What don't I know about you that I should?" or "What skills do you have that could make you do this job well?"

# PUZZLE AND LOGIC QUESTIONS

## 81. PUZZLE AND LOGIC QUESTION #1

A snail wants to reach the top of a light pole: every day it goes up 4 meters, but every night it slides down by 3. How many days does it take to reach the top of the pole, which is 7 meters high?

**Answer:** The question is a pitfall: the snail, net of ascent and descent, goes up a meter every day, so the first answer that would be given is 7 days for 7 meters ... but it's wrong! In fact, already the fourth day he manages to reach the top! Think out loud, and don't worry even if you give a wrong answer: for the examiner, it's a good way to see how you deal with mistakes!

## 82. PUZZLE AND LOGIC QUESTION #2

You have a 5-liter jug and a 3-liter jug. That's great, but how would you measure out exactly 4 liters without using any other equipment?

**ANSWER**: First, fill the 3-liter jug and pour it into the 5-liter jug. The 3-liter jug is now empty, and the 5-liter jug has 3 liters in it. Now, fill the 3-liter jug again and tip it slowly into the 5-liter jug. You'll have 2 liters in before the 5-liter jug is full because it already has 3 liters in from before?

Now you have 1 liter left in the 3-liter jug and the 5-liter jug is full. Empty the 5-liter jug. Now pour the remaining 1 liter in the 3-liter jug into the 5-liter jug.

Lastly, fill up the 3-liter jug again and tip it all into the 5-liter jug, which now ends up with exactly four liters in it!

## 83. PUZZLE AND LOGIC QUESTION #3

You're about to board a train from London to New Jersey. You want to know if it's raining, so you call your three friends who live in New Jersey. Each friend has a 2/3 chance of telling you the truth and a 1/3 chance of telling you a lie. All three friends tell you that, yes, it's raining in New Jersey. What is the probability that it is, in fact, raining in New Jersey?

**Answer:** The answer is 96%. You only need one friend to be telling the truth. So if you calculate the odds of them all lying, that's 1/3 multiplied together, making 1/27 (1/3 x 1/3 x 1/3).

So that's a 1 in 27 chance that all of your three friends are lying. So, switch that around, and it's a 26/27 chance one of them is telling the truth – or 96% - that it is, indeed raining in New jersey!

## 84. PUZZLE AND LOGIC QUESTION#4

You are on the surface of the earth, and walk a mile to the south, one to the west, one to the north, and find yourself exactly where you started. Where are you?

**Answer:** There are two answers to this question: "The short answer? Are you either at the North Pole or somewhere near the South Pole! The long answer? If you depart from the North Pole, and follow the instructions, in practice do three sides of a triangle, returning to the starting point, because the Earth is a sphere. Instead of the answer of the South Pole, it's more complicated: you have to find a circumference of a mile with the center exactly in the Pole, and then start walking from a point that is a mile north of the circumference you have identified. So with the mile south, you get to the circumference, with the mile to the west you go around the entire circumference, and with the mile to the north, you return to the starting point.

## 85. PUZZLE AND LOGIC QUESTION#5

If a pencil and an eraser cost $ 1 and 10 cents, and the pencil costs $ 1 more than the rubber, how much does the rubber cost?

**Answer:** 10 cents No, stop! Reflect. If it were that easy, they wouldn't have asked you, so it's probably the wrong answer. In fact it is so: the right answer is ... 5 cents ($ 1.05 + $ 0.05 = $ 1.10)!

## 86. PUZZLE AND LOGIC QUESTION#6

In a watch, how many times do the hour and minute hands overlap, within 24 hours?

**Answer:** How important it is to wear the analog watch on your wrist during the job interview! But in any case you can't wait to verify it by actually checking the hands, so the answer is 22, counting to believe!

## 87. PUZZLE AND LOGIC QUESTION#7

You are in a room with 3 switches. Each switch turns on an oven, located on the upper floor. How do you know which switch turns on which oven, being able to go upstairs only once?

**Answer:** In questions of logic of this kind, the best thing to do is to ask questions, and reason aloud. If you shut up, whoever is in front of you does not understand if you are going in the right direction, or if you are groping in the dark; in either case, he will have no way to help you. For this specific question, you find the answer by thinking about the fact that an oven, when it is turned on, gets hot. So you can understand the matching oven-switch if you turn on two ovens for a while and then turn off one. Finally, you turn on the last one: when you go upstairs, you'll find an oven that is off and cold (the switch you didn't touch), an oven turned off but warm ( switch that you turned on and then turned off) and a hot, lit oven (the third switch).

## 88. PUZZLE AND LOGIC QUESTION#8

You must cut a birthday cake into eight identical parts, but it has only 3 cuts available. How do you do?

**Answer**: But how, do you have a self-destructing knife after you use it three times? Why did you buy something like that? This would be a smart question but forget it, it's not worth it! Therefore, remaining in the initial hypotheses, it is quite immediate to understand how to do it: with two perpendicular cuts you cut the cake into four identical pieces. And then? With the last shot of the knife, cut the cake in half horizontally: this way the pieces become eight, and the knife can explode happy to have reached its goal.

## 89. PUZZLE AND LOGIC QUESTION#9

You wake up and find 1000 emails to read, but you have time to read-only 100. What do you do?

Answer: I turn off my cell phone, computer, and brain and go back to sleep. When I wake up I will not even have time to read one, and I will have solved the problem! It could be a solution, except that when you wake up you probably won't even have a job. What do you do, do you read one every ten? Unfortunately, luck is not by your side, and it is not something to rely on. Answer trying to prioritize conversations: perhaps by selecting the addresses that you know are the most important, or by searching for a certain word in the titles, or by reading only the answers to conversations already started.

## 90. PUZZLE AND LOGIC QUESTION#10

You are in a dark room, with 50 black and 50 white stockings: how many stockings should you take as a minimum to make sure you go out and have a pair of socks of the same color?

**Answer:** Surely if you take 51 stockings, when you go out you're sure to have a pair of the same color, but it's not the lowest number you can find! Let's think: when you take a sock, it's one color. When you take the second one, it can be the same colour or the opposite color. But when you take the third one, it's a pair with one of the two previous stockings: the answer is 3!

## 91. PUZZLE AND LOGIC QUESTION#11

There are 3 boxes, one is full only of apples, the second one of oranges only, the third contains both apples and oranges. They have been badly labeled, and no box contains what the label says. You can open only one crate without looking inside, and from the crate, you have chosen you can extract only one fruit. By doing this, you need to be able to understand what's in the various boxes. How do you do?

**Answer:** A little more complex than others, but not impossible. The central point of this puzzle is which case you decide to open. In fact, you have to take a fruit from the chest labeled as "mixed fruit": since the label is false, the content will only be the type of fruit you take out. If you take out an apple, the crate will only have apples. So the crate labeled as "only oranges" must necessarily have mixed fruit, and the last crate will be just orange - and if you pull out an orange, follow the same reasoning and you will get the answer.

## 92. PUZZLE AND LOGIC QUESTION #12

How many golf balls can be on a school bus?

**Answer:** It is one of the questions that has spread the most since the Google interviews, it has also been among those that have contributed to the fashion of the "brainteaser" questions in job interviews - especially in talks for IT jobs. In fact, it is an absurd question, which does not require the right answer: what it requires is reasoning, which is valid and logical. (Not even those who ask you this question know how many balls there can be on the school bus!) Then give them what they ask you: think aloud, explain what you would do, use a pen and paper, and try to hypothesize an answer, without saying the first number that comes to mind! You will reason on the average size of a school bus (length and height), so you will find the volume. Then you hypnotize how many seats a school bus may have, and how much value they may take. Then you almost know the volume of a golf ball and you good to go.

## 93. PUZZLE AND LOGIC QUESTION #13

In a country in which people only want boys, every family continues to have children until they have a boy. If they have a girl, they have another child. If they have a boy, they stop. What is the proportion of boys to girls in the country?

**Answer**: Following is the required calculation:

Expected Number of boys for 1 family = 1*(Probability of 1 boy) + 1*(Probability of 1 girl and a boy) + 1*(Probability of 2 girls and a boy) + ...

For C couples = 1*(C*1/2) + 1*(C*1/2*1/2) + 1*(C*1/2*1/2*1/2) + ...

Expected Number of boys = C/2 + C/4 + C/8 + C/16 + ...

Expected Number of boys = C

Expected Number of girls for 1 family = 0*(Probability of 0 girls) + 1*(Probability of 1 girl and a boy) + 2*(Probability of 2 girls and a boy) + ...

For C couples = 0*(C*1/2) + 1*(C*1/2*1/2) + 2*(C*1/2*1/2*1/2) + ...

Expected Number of girls = 0 + C/4 + 2*C/8 + 3*C/16 + ...

Expected Number of girls = C

Therefore, the proportion is C/C = 1:1

## 94. PUZZLE AND LOGIC QUESTION #14

You have 10 bags full of coins. In each bag are infinite coins. But one bag is full of forgeries, and you can't remember which one. But you do know that genuine coins weigh 1 gram, but forgeries weigh 1.1 grams. You have to identify that bag in minimum readings. You are provided with a digital weighing machine.

**Answer:** Take 1 coin from the first bag, 2 coins from the second bag, 3 coins from the third bag and so on. Eventually, we'll get 55 (1+2+3...+9+10) coins. Now, weigh all the 55 coins together. Depending on the resulting weighing machine reading, you can find which bag has the forged coins such that if the reading ends with 0.4 then it is the 4th bag, if it ends with 0.7 then it is the 7th bag and so on.

## 95. PUZZLE AND LOGIC QUESTION #15

There are 100 prisoners all sentenced to death. One night before the execution, the warden gives them a chance to live if they all work on a strategy together. The execution scenario is as follows. On the day of execution, all the prisoners will be made to stand in a straight line such that one prisoner stands just behind another and so on. All prisoners will be wearing a hat either of

Blue color or Red. The prisoners don't know what color of hat they are wearing. The prisoner who is standing at the last can see all the prisoners in front of him (and what color of hat they are wearing). A prisoner can see all the hats in front of him. The prisoner who is standing in the front of the line cannot see anything. The executioner will ask each prisoner what color of hat they are wearing one by one, starting from the last in the line. The prisoner can only speak "Red" or "Blue". He cannot say anything else. If he gets it right, he lives otherwise he is shot instantly. All the prisoners standing in front of him can hear the answers and gunshots. Assuming that the prisoners are intelligent and would stick to the plan, what strategy would the prisoners makeover the night to minimize the number of deaths?

**Answer:** The strategy is that the last person will say 'red' if the number of red hats in front of him is odd and 'blue' if the number of red hats in front of him is even. Now, the 99th guy will see them if the red hats in front of him are odd or even. If it is odd then obviously the hat above him is blue, else it is red. From now on, it's pretty intuitive.

## 96. PUZZLE AND LOGIC QUESTION #16

You are in a dark room where a table is kept. There are 50 coins placed on the table, out of which 10 coins are showing tails and 40 coins are showing heads. The task is to divide this set of 50 coins into 2 groups (not necessarily the same size) such that both groups have the same number of coins showing the tails.

**ANSWER:** Divide the group into two groups of 40 coins and 10 coins. Flip all coins of the group with 10 coins.

## 97. PUZZLE AND LOGIC QUESTION#17

You have two sand timers, which can show 4 minutes and 7 minutes respectively. Use both the sand timers(at a time or one after another or any other combination) and measure a time of 9 minutes.

**Answer:**

- Start the 7-minute sand timer and the 4-minute sand timer.
- Once the 4-minute sand timer ends to turn it upside-down instantly.
- Once the 7-minute sand timer ends to turn it upside-down instantly.
- After the 4-minute sand timer ends turn the 7-minute sand timer upside down(it has now minute of sand in it)
- So effectively 8 + 1 = 9.

## 98. PUZZLE AND LOGIC QUESTION#18

There is a bus with 100 labeled seats (labeled from 1 to 100). There are 100 persons standing in a queue. Persons are also labeled from 1 to 100. People board on the bus in sequence from 1 to n. The rule is, if a person 'I' boards the bus, he checks if seat 'I' is empty. If it is empty, he sits there, else he randomly picks an empty seat and sit there. Given that 1st person picks seats randomly, find the probability that the 100th person sits on his place i.e. 100th seat.

**Answer:** The final answer is the probability that the last person ends in up in his proper seat is exactly ½

The reasoning goes as follows:

First, observe that the fate of the last person is determined the moment either the first or the last seat is selected! This is because the last person will either get the first seat or the last seat. Any other seat will necessarily be taken by the time the last guy gets to 'choose'. Since at each choice step, the first or last is equally probable to be taken, the last person will get either the first or last with equal probability: 1/2.

## 99. PUZZLE AND LOGIC QUESTION#19

There are 10 incredibly smart boys at school: A, B, C, D, E, F, G, H, I and Sam. They run into class laughing at 8:58 am, just two minutes before the playtime ends and are stopped by a stern-looking teacher: Mr. Rabbit. sees that A, B, C, and D have mud on their faces. He, being a teacher who thinks that his viewpoint is always correct and acts only to enforce rules rather than thinking about the world that should be, lashes out at the poor kids. "Silence!", he shouts. "Nobody will talk. All of you who have mud on your faces, get out of the class!". The kids look at each other. Each kid could see whether the other kids had mud on their faces, but could not see his own face. Nobody goes out of the class. "I said, all of you who have mud on your faces, get out of the class!" Still, nobody leaves. After trying 5 more times, the bell rings at 9 and Mr. Rabbit exasperatedly yells: "I can clearly see that at least one of you kids has mud on his face!". The kids grin, knowing that their ordeal will be over soon. Sure enough, after a few more times bawling of "All of you who have mud on your faces, get out of the class!", A, B, C, and D walk out of the class. Explain how A, B, C, and D knew that they had mud on their faces. What made the kids grin? Everybody knew that there was at least one kid with mud on his face. Support with a logical statement that a kid did not know before Mr. Rabbit's exasperated yell at 9, but that the kid knew right after it.

**Answer:** After Mr. Rabbit's first shout, they understood that at least one boy has mud on his face. So, if it was exactly one boy, then the boy would know that he had mud on his face and go out after one shouting.

Since nobody went out after one shouting, they understood that at least two boys have mud on their faces. If it were exactly two boys, those boys would know (they would see only one other's muddy face and they'd understand their face is muddy too) and go out after the next shouting.

Since nobody went out after the second shouting, it means there are at least three muddy faces And so on, after the fourth shouting, A, B, C, and D would go out of the class.

This explanation does leave some questions open. Everybody knew at least three others had mud on their faces, why did they have to wait for Mr. Rabbit's shout at the first place? Why did they have to go through all four shoutings after that as well?

In multi-agent reasoning, an important concept arises of common knowledge. Everybody knows that there are at least three muddy faces but they cannot act together on that information without knowing that everybody else knows that too. And that everybody knows that and so on. This is what we'll be analyzing. It requires some imagination, so be prepared.

A knows that B, C, and D have mud on their faces. A does not know if B knows that three people have mud on their faces. A knows that B knows that two people have mud on their faces. But A can't expect people to act on that information because A does not know if B knows that C knows that there are two people with mud on their faces. If you think this is all uselessly complicated, consider this:

A can imagine a world in which he does not have mud on his face. (Call this world A) In A's world, A can imagine B having a world where both A and B do not have mud on their faces. (Call this world AB)

A can imagine a world where B imagines that C imagines that D imagines that nobody has mud on their faces. (Call this world ABCD). So when Mr. Rabbit shouted initially, it could have been that nobody was going out because a world ABCD was possible in which nobody should be going out anyway.

So here's a statement that changes after Mr. Rabbit's yell. World ABCD is not possible i.e. A cannot imagine a world where B imagines that C imagines that D imagines that nobody has mud on their faces. So now in world ABC, D knows he has mud on his face. And in world ABD, C knows he has mud on his face and so on.

# FINAL QUESTION

## 100. DO YOU HAVE ANY QUESTION FOR ME?

Never say "no" as this is perhaps the worst response ever given by any interview candidate! Remember that interviews are not integrations but are business conversations where both the parties should ask and respond to questions. This is probably your very first chance during the interview, to ask a question. Questioning will indicate that as a fresher, you came well-prepared for the interview and you are still absorbed in the conversation. It will also show that you do take an interest in the organization. Make a general list of five questions about the company and ask them to your Interviewer, after all, other HR interview questions and answers are over. Coming back to the situation, the best answer for a fresher is as follows:

"How has your journey been so far in this organization? What excites you the most about working here? How long does it ideally take a person to prove their caliber here? Where is the organization headed in the next years? What are the next steps of this interview?"

**OR**

"You've provided a thorough overview of the role. One thing I was wondering was whether employees have the opportunity to pursue professional development opportunities, like attending conferences or taking an online class to develop their skill sets

# THINGS YOU SHOULD NEVER SAY IN A JOB INTERVIEW

In an interview, your primary goal is to get across to the hiring manager why you above all the other candidates are the right person for the job. That you have the right set of skills, a great personality, and the drive to really make things happen in your new role. But as you're preparing answers to interview questions that'll let you do all of those things, it's equally important to know what the hiring manager will consider a red flag. After all, a wrong move or two, and it won't matter how great your sales numbers at your last job were. To help you out, steer clear of these 30 messages. You'll make sure that your awesome abilities and accomplishment.

## "Tell Me What You Do Around Here"

You never want to walk into an interview knowing next to nothing about the position or company—you want to show that you're excited enough that you've done some homework and thought about how you'd fit in. To get started, do some online research, and try to find a current or past employee you can talk to before the big day.

## "I Didn't Get Along With My Boss"

You don't want to speak negatively about anyone you've worked within the past. Even if a previous manager could put the characters in Horrible Bosses to shame, your interviewer doesn't know that and could wonder whether you're the difficult one to work with.

## "I'm Really Nervous"

Even if you're more nervous than you've ever been, no company wants to hire someone who lacks confidence. "So, in this case, honesty is not the best policy,"

## "I'll Do Whatever"

Most hiring managers are looking for people who are incredibly passionate about the role they're taking on. So when you say something to the effect of, "I don't care what jobs you have available, I'll do anything!" that's a big red flag. Instead, target your search to a specific role at each company, and be ready to explain why it's exactly what you're looking for.

# "I Know I Don't Have Much Experience, But…"

This mistake is easy to make, especially if you're a recent grad or career changer. Problem is, when you apologize for the experience you don't have, you're essentially saying that you're not a great hire, that you're not quite the right fit for the role, or even that you would be starting from square one. And that's just not the case! Instead of drawing attention to your weaknesses, stay positive, focus on your strengths, and immediately launch into your transferable skills and infectious enthusiasm for the position.

# "Perfectionism Is My Greatest Weakness"

Here's the thing: Chances are, telling a hiring manager that perfectionism is your greatest weakness won't surprise him or her and it might come off as sounding like an overly rehearsed cliché. It also doesn't offer much of a true insight into your work style or personality especially if half the other candidates are giving the same response. Try a more genuine response

## "It's on My Resume"

If a recruiter is asking you about a certain skill, don't reference your resume, and instead, use it as your moment to shine. "Here's the thing; I know it's on your resume, but if I'm asking you about a particular job or experience, I want you to tell me more beyond a written word. I'm actually evaluating your communication and social skills. Are you articulate? Should you be client-facing, or are you someone we need to keep hidden in the basement next to the IT lending library?

## "I Think Outside the Box"

Skip these overused business phrases, and describe your skills and abilities using stories about things you've actually done.

## "I'd Like to Start My Own Business as Soon as Possible"

Entrepreneurial ambitions are great, but if you're applying for a job to work for someone else, you probably want to downplay the fact that you're trying to get funding for your burgeoning startup. Most employers want to hire people who are going to be around for a while, and if there's any suspicion that you're just collecting a paycheck until you can do your own thing, you probably won't get the job.

## "How Much Vacation Time Do I Get?"

When you bust out with an immediate litany of WIIFM (what's in it for me?) questions, you look both arrogant and, frankly, unappealing. Guess what interviewers want to know when they meet with you? First and foremost, they want to know what you can do for them. What can you do to make that company money, improve business processes, grow the organization and, importantly, make their lives easier? Making you happy will be important if they want you, but you're not even going to get to that stage if you make your list of demands clear too early.

## "I Know I Don't Have Much Experience, But..."

This mistake is easy to make, especially if you're a recent grad or career changer. Problem is, when you apologize for the experience you don't have, you're essentially saying that you're not a great hire, that you're not quite the right fit for the role, or even that you would be starting from square one. And that's just not the case! Instead of drawing attention to your weaknesses, stay positive, focus on your strengths, and immediately launch into your transferable skills and infectious enthusiasm for the position.

## "Yes! I Have a Great Answer for That!"

Practiced your answers to some interview questions? Great. But don't memorize them word for word. When you're hyper-prepared and hanging on the edge of your seat waiting for certain questions for which you've prepared to be asked, you will likely have a very hard time engaging in genuine conversation with the interviewer. And interviewers don't tend to hire detached people who can't seem to have a genuine conversation. Certainly, walk-in prepared, but force yourself to not memorize or over-rehearse the practice questions.

## "How Soon Do You Promote Employees?"

An individual asking this question may come off as arrogant and entitled. A better way to ask this? "I'm really interested in staying at a place for a while. What do career paths within the company typically look like?"

## "Sorry, I'm So Late."

Just be on time. Enough said

# HOW TO APPEAR CONFIDENT IN AN INTERVIEW

Projecting confidence in a job interview can be just as important as showing your skills and demonstrating your unique qualifications. It is important to practice the way you communicate confidence and professionalism, as this can improve your performance in the room as well as calm your nerves. Confidence is the act of trusting yourself. During a job interview, showing that you trust yourself is critical because it can lead your interviewer to trust in you, as well. Aim to communicate to your interviewer that you know you can do this job well. However, it is normal to feel nervous when interviewing, so try to take some time to practice how to appear confident before your meeting.

Use these tips to impress interviewers with your confidence:

## Make eye contact

To show confidence, start by practicing your eye contact. Keeping natural and steady eye contact throughout your interview is an excellent way to project confidence. Aim to maintain natural eye contact instead of making eye contact that feels intense or prolonged. Try occasionally looking at your resume or other material you brought with you to the interview before turning your attention back to the hiring manager.

## Maintain good posture

After you work on your eye contact, you might also find it helpful to practice good posture. Body language is an important aspect of communicating confidence during your interview. Start by sitting with your arms unfolded in your lap in order to convey an open, friendly attitude. Make your back straight with your shoulders back and your chest and chin raised.

Pro-tip: Standing with your feet shoulder-width apart, chest and chin high, back straight and your fists on your waist for a few minutes before your interview can make you feel calmer and confident.

## Practice your handshake

One great way to show confidence in an interview is to greet the interviewer with a firm handshake. A firm handshake shows experience and confidence, and it gives the interviewer a good first impression. Keep the following tips in mind to give a good handshake

- The interviewer should be the one to initiate the handshake
- Stand and look the interviewer in the eye when you shake hands
- Offer a sincere smile to show you are happy to be there
- If your palm is damp, quickly blot it on the side of your pants or skirt before shaking hands
- Greet the person with her name and a pleasantry, such as, "It is very nice to meet you, Ms. Smith"
- Have a firm handshake, but do not apply too much force
- The handshake should last between two and five seconds, which usually equals two or three pumps
- Make sure your other hand is visible and unclenched.

## Practice breathing techniques

When you get nervous, the blood flows away from your brain and into your muscles for fight or flight mode. This lack of blood in the brain can impact cognitive functions. However, when you take slow, deep breaths, you bring oxygen back to your brain to help you think.

For the most effective breathing technique to calm your nerves, follow these steps:

- Take a deep breath in through your nose
- Try to take in enough air to feel your stomach expand
- Slowly exhale through your mouth
- Repeat this process three times, and focus on centering your thoughts while you are exhaling

## Calm your fidgeting

Fidgeting is a sign of nervousness. If you tend to tap your fingers or twirl your hair, practice keeping your hands on the table. You should also make a point not to keep a pen or paper in your hands if you typically fidget with anything you are holding. If you often shake your leg when you are nervous, you can keep your hands in your lap and apply a little pressure to remind yourself to stop shaking. Try asking a friend or family member to tell you how you fidget so you can be aware of your habits and work on them.

## Prepare and rehearse your answers

One great way to showcase interview confidence is to prepare your answers to common interview questions. When you walk into an interview with the knowledge that you are prepared, it can take off the pressure and help you feel more confident. Consider sitting down with a friend or family member to think about your answers. They do not need to be memorized but aim to prepare enough so that you can produce responses you are proud of.

## Talk slowly

Speak calmly and slowly. To stop yourself from rambling, try to answer each question by addressing one point at a time. Confident people also tend to take their time when answering questions. If you feel like you need a moment to compose your thoughts, feel free to say, "That is a good question. Let me think about that for a second." Also, do not be afraid to ask the interviewer for clarification of the question.

## Dress the part

Choosing the right outfit for your interview can help improve your confidence. Research the company's dress code to see how you should dress for the interview. If the dress code is formal, men should wear a suit, and women should consider a pantsuit or skirt suit. Look for clothing in classic and neutral colors, such as black, navy or brown. If the company is casual, proper interview attire can include slacks, dark jeans, button-up shirts, and polo shirts. When in doubt, it is wise to dress more formally.

## Think positively

A final way to calm your nerves and boost your confidence is to think positively. One step you can take to think positively is to focus on areas where you lack confidence and practice making them better. Areas of low confidence can include:

- Shaking hands with the interviewer
- Starting the interview
- Beginning to speak
- Answering questions

Once you pinpoint where you feel most nervous, you can make a plan on how to address these areas. To work on the previous examples you can:

- Practice shaking hands with friends
- Sit down for mock interviews with family
- Record your mock interviews to review them
- Practice answering different types of interview questions

# CONCLUSION

The interview is by far the most subjective part of the hiring process and therefore is probably the most complex. There is no one-size-fits-all prescription for effective interviewing; each interviewer can only learn the techniques and decide for themselves which combination proves most successful for hiring a given position. Most interviewers don't choose one technique, style, or format and use it exclusively; rather they'll pick and choose from the various methods and create an interview process that works for them. Perhaps they'll use Directive or Structured questions during the initial phone screen interview, then ease into the face-to-face interview with some Traditional questions followed by Behavioural – prompting the candidate to provide specifics through SOARA or STAR-based questions. Certain roles may benefit from incorporating the Case interview technique, and for a few positions, perhaps an intense sales role, the Stress interview may prove particularly revealing.

But perhaps the most important part of interviewing isn't the technique or style used, but rather the preparation beforehand and the grading system after. Thinking through exactly which skills and traits are desired for the position will help the interviewer to focus on what's most relevant during the interview. After the interview, rating the candidate using an established scale allows hiring managers to more fairly assess candidates and ultimately, make better hiring decisions. Interviews are great tools that help both the company and the candidates to make the right selection for the jobs. Interview not only helps the establishment to prosper and grow by selecting the right candidates but it also provides a way for the employee to grow both professionally and personally.

Printed in Poland
by Amazon Fulfillment
Poland Sp. z o.o., Wrocław